Edmund Martin Geldart

Folk-lore of Modern Greece

The Tales of the People

Edmund Martin Geldart

Folk-lore of Modern Greece
The Tales of the People

ISBN/EAN: 9783744778817

Printed in Europe, USA, Canada, Australia, Japan

Cover: Foto ©Thomas Meinert / pixelio.de

More available books at **www.hansebooks.com**

FOLK-LORE

OF

MODERN GREECE:

THE TALES OF THE PEOPLE.

EDITED BY THE

Rev. E. M. GELDART, M.A.,

AUTHOR OF "THE MODERN GREEK LANGUAGE IN ITS RELATION TO ANCIENT
GREEK;" "A GUIDE TO MODERN GREEK," &c., &c.

LONDON:

W. SWAN SONNENSCHEIN & CO.,

PATERNOSTER SQUARE.

1884.

PRINTED BY
KELLY AND CO., GATE STREET, LINCOLN'S INN FIELDS;
AND KINGSTON-ON-THAMES.

PREFACE.

THE following Fairy Tales are translated, with the exception of
the first three, the originals of which are contained in the
Parnassos, a journal published by the Philological Society of that
name in Athens, from the Greek text, edited by J. Pio at
Copenhagen, under the title : *Contes Populaires Grecs publiés
d'après les Manuscrits du Dr. J. G. de Hahn*, 1879. Von Hahn
himself, the author of *Albanesische Studien*, Jena, 1854, and
Griechische und albanesische Märchen, Leipzig, 1864, having lived
from his youth in various parts of Greece, had employed native
amanuenses to write down, by word of mouth, the several stories
which formed the basis of his German version, as they fell from
the lips of their narrators. Some of these were subsequently
revised by Professor Mavrophrydes, of Athens, the rest after his
death by M. Pio, the editor of the Greek text already mentioned.
Of many of the tales the latter found duplicate versions among
the posthumous MSS. of Von Hahn, and, by the collation of
these, he succeeded in producing a text which, while it leaves
much to be desired from a purely philological point of view, is
evidently, as the mere style of the recital sufficiently attests, a
far closer approximation to genuine oral tradition than is mostly
the case with collections of popular legends. With regard to my
own work, namely, the selection and translation of the tales contained in the present volume, I wish to say first that I have
confined myself entirely to those of which I had the Greek text
before me ; secondly, that I have translated them directly from
the original, and subsequently compared, where I could, the
German version of Von Hahn : besides consulting native Greek

friends on doubtful points. I cannot, however, ask to be
judged by Von Hahn's translation. Great as his merit is in
having first drawn the attention of his countrymen to the rich
treasure of fairy legends (in a prose form) to be found in Greece,
he was rather a mythologist than a linguist, and his German
version is not only free, but in some instances either demonstrably
inaccurate or founded on a different reading to that followed by
Pio. In regard to the choice I have made within the limits
assigned, and resisting the temptation to enlarge the present
volume either from those portions of Von Hahn's *Märchen* of
which the Greek text is not published, or from the charming
French collection of Emile Legrand: *Recueil de Contes Populaires
Grecs*, Paris, 1881, of which also the original is not yet accessible,
I have to say that I was still further restricted in the matter of
selection, by the character of the legends themselves, many of
which exhibit all that naïve unconsciousness of the proprieties of
civilized life, which belongs to popular thought and speech, and
which, while wholly innocent in itself, renders the narratives un-
presentable in polite society, except at the cost of such mutilation
as would deprive them of scientific value. For this scientific
value consists essentially, as it seems to me, in the faithful and
rigorous preservation both of the matter and the form of the
original, so far as this is possible and compatible with translation.
I have therefore not sought nor desired to remove the uncouth
abruptness of the narrative, or to make it in any sense conform
to the demands of literary elegance; I have rather endeavoured
to retain, so far as the English idiom at all admits, even the rapid
transition from the past tense to the historic present, and *vice versâ*,
which is so specially characteristic of popular oral narration, and
have left intact, as far as I could, the somewhat confusing inter-
calation of comment, and often far-fetched proverbial allusion
and illustration, which is another strongly marked trait of these
vernacular recitals. The main interest for the student attaching
to these tales centres around the problem of the migration of

myths. Many an old nursery favourite will be recognised through its Greek disguise by English children when they read, as I hope they will read, this book. A little girl of eleven interrupted me in the story of the Two Brothers and the Forty-Nine Dragons by the cry, "Why that's the tale of Ali Baba and the Forty Thieves!" And so it is, with a difference. How far such tales are *indogermanishes Gemeingut*, how far they have crept into Greece through Turkish, Arabic and perhaps, ultimately, Persian sources; what way they have travelled, and what they have lost and gained upon the journey, is one of the most interesting, and at the same time complicated questions which can engage the investigator of ethnological relations. That Little Saddleslut is the Greek Cinderella is obvious at the first blush. But why the one sat upon the hearth and the other on a saddle, not without a reminiscence of the hearth in respect of the place of burial of her much injured mother; why in Greece the corpse of the mother replaces the Godmother of the Teutonic legend, whether or not in the spinning wheel and the cannibal feast which usher in the Greek story, we have elements purely Hellenic, in a word, to account at once for difference and likeness in the two tales when placed side by side : these are among the most knotty points which savants can undertake to determine. The reader who is curious about parallels will find abundant comparative illustration in the notes to Von Hahn's collection. But the inexhaustible nature of the inquiry here opened up deters me under present conditions, especially that of my own ignorance, from doing more than offering one or two solitary and perhaps superfluous hints. With the story of "The Golden Steed" compare "Der gute Johannes" in Grimm's *Kinder- und Hausmärchen.* With " Starbright and Birdie," Grimm's " Brüderchen und Schwesterchen!" With " Sir Lazarus and the Dragons," Grimm's " Das tapfere Schneiderlein." Again, as essentially the same tale in another form, compare "The Man without a Beard" and " Der Riese und der Schneider." I venture here to

hazard the suggestion that the greater prominence of solar
and stellar elements to be found in the Greek, compared with
the German versions, of cognate stories, points to a higher
antiquity for the former, as regards the shape in which they have
come down. I would especially refer to the almost total disappear-
ance of the astronomical "strain" in "Brüderchen and Schwesterchen," and its, even conscious, presence in the story of
"Starbright and Birdie." For a more distinctly solar signification I
would draw special attention to the adventures of the "Scab-
pate," pp. 56-65, and 152-181. His tumbling in the mire, his
horses of various hue, his javelin wherewith he slays his rival in
the first story, and all the varied vicissitudes of his chequered
fortune, are so many ways of representing the struggle of the sun
with clouds and darkness, and depicting its final victory over
storm and gloom. In the "Tale of the Dragon," pp. 141-143, the
part played by the pea reminds us curiously of Hans Andersen's
story of "The Real Princess."

CONTENTS.

THE TWO BROTHERS AND THE FORTY-NINE DRAGONS.

(SYRA.)

——:o:——

ONCE upon a time there were two brothers. One was very rich and had four children, the other was very poor and had seven children. One day the poor man's wife went to the rich man and said to him, "I am very wretched, for I have not enough bread for my children. I take a little meal and I mix it with a great deal of bran and so manage to make bread. It is well nigh a year since my children have had any relish with their meals; they get nothing but bread and water."

He answered her: "And yet your children are so strong, while mine, with all their feeding and the comforts they enjoy, are always ailing!"

The poor woman said, "God has given us poverty and hunger, but thanks be to Heaven, our children are hale and hearty. Now, therefore, I have come to beg you, if you have any work, not to send for any one but me, so may God send health to your children!" and as she spoke these words, the tears ran from her eyes like a river.

Then he called his wife and said to her:

"Have we any work for her to come and do for us daily, so that she may not sit idle?"

His wife answered him: "Let her come twice a week and knead bread for us."

When she heard these words she was glad, for she thought at once, that when she kneaded that fine white bread they would give her some of it, and her poor children would eat and rejoice. So she rose to go away. And they said to her:

"Good-bye, and remember to come to-morrow morning."

B

Thus they bade her farewell without giving her a scrap of anything. As she set off home she said to herself, "Would that I were rich, that I might open my cupboard, and bring forth a bit of cheese, or a piece of bread, or at least a little rice, or such like household store to gladden the hearts of the poor!" and lifting her hands to heaven she said: "Why, oh my God, hast thou made me so poor?"

And so she went weeping home where her children were waiting for her ever so eagerly, hoping she might bring them something.

But alas, poor thing, she came with empty hands.

The next day she went very early in the morning to the rich man's house to knead bread, and when she had kneaded it and ended her work, they bade her farewell and told her to be sure and come next time, without giving her so much as a cup of cold water.

As soon as she came home the children said to her:

"Have you brought us anything, mother?"

"No!" she said: "may be, when they have done baking they will send us a bit of bread."

But in vain she waited, and when evening came not a loaf nor a plate of anything to eat appeared.

In two or three days they sent word for her to come and knead again: for they liked her kneading much. Then the poor woman arose and went again; and as she was kneading the thought came into her head, not to wash her hands till she got home, and then to wash them in a dish, and to give the wash to her children instead of plain water. So as soon as she had done kneading, she hurried away, and when she got home she said to her children, "Wait till I give you a little milk-soup." And washing her hands well of the dough, she filled a good dish, and gave each one a little to drink.

And they liked it so much that they said, "Mother, whenever you go to knead, mind you bring us some of that broth to drink."

A month passed while she went on at this work. And it seems that God blessed her children, for they grew fatter than ever.

house, he put his head in at the door and said, "How do you do here?" Then he turns and looks at all the children, and is amazed to see how fat they seem; and going out at the door in a rage, he went home to his wife and called her: "Come here and tell me what you give to my sister-in-law who comes to knead for us."

Now she was frightened at the way he shouted at her and said, "I never gave her anything yet, because I am so afraid of giving her too much and your scolding me."

Says he, "You must have given her something, for her children are so fat they look as if they would burst."

Then she swore an oath and said, "She takes nothing away with her but her unwashed hands and she washes them at home, and gives the wash to her children to drink."

When he heard that he said, "Put a stop to that too."

So the next day when the woman went to knead, her mistress waited until she had finished, and when she had done, said to her, "Wash your hands well and then go."

When the poor woman heard that her countenance fell, and she quailed with grief to think how she should go to her children, and they would beg the milk-soup of her. When she came to her house her children were gathered together awaiting her, and as soon as they saw her come in they all cried with one voice :

"What have you got, mother?"

"Nothing, children; I forgot myself and washed my hands!"

All the children began to weep and to cry, "How could you so forget us, as not to bring us that beautiful broth?"

While they were thus weeping and wailing, the father entered the house and said, "What ails the children that they cry?"

Then she told him all that had happened, and he was sorely grieved, and made up his mind to kill himself, and so that his wife might not guess his purpose, he asked her for a bag to go to the hill and gather herbs. She gave it him, and he went away. And as he wandered about bewildered for a long while, he found himself at the top of a high crag, and there he made up his mind to fling himself down and die. Then he spied facing the crag a great castle, and he said to himself, "Before I kill myself, I may as well go and see what that castle is like."

And drawing near he saw a tree, and he climbed up into it to see who lived in the castle. After a little while he looked, and behold, a number of dragons came out! He counted them, and they were forty-nine. When the dragons were gone, they left the door open, for that was always their custom. So he climbed down from the tree and went into the castle and walked about it, and saw that it contained much treasure. Then he took his bag and filled it with as much as his back could carry, and went away at once, for he feared lest the dragons should catch him.

When they came back they perceived that a thief had been and stolen some of their money, and from henceforth they determined that one of them should always stay behind in the castle. The poor man returned to the town two days later, and found his wife weeping and refusing to be comforted, for she feared that his affliction had led him to go and kill himself. But when she saw him come back she praised God because he came alive. Then said her husband to her, "Wife, God has taken pity on our children and on you, who made bread so long at my brother's house, though they never gave you a morsel to feed our little ones. See, here we have enough to live for some time." And opening his bag he showed her the coins.

She was a pious woman, so she said, "The first thing you must buy is some oil that we may light a lamp to our Lady, which we have not done for so long."

And her husband hearkened unto her and straightway went and bought oil, and when they had lighted the lamp they prayed with all their hearts and with tears in their eyes.

The next day her husband arose, and the first thing he did was to buy a house; and he moved into it with his homely furniture and his poor children.

On the first evening he said to his wife, "From day to day we will buy what we want for the house, but nothing more, for we must bear in mind how you used to give milk-soup to the children to drink, to save them from dying of hunger."

"Yes," said she, "I will never ask you for anything that we do not want."

Two months passed during which these people lived happily. They did nothing else but go to church and help the poor. One

day, then, the wife of the rich man came to visit her poor kins-
woman, for she had heard from many that she was now well off,
and she herself had begun to suffer misfortune; all her sheep
had died, her fields had brought forth no crops, the frost had
bitten many of her trees, and she had met with many other mis-
haps. When the poor woman saw her without being in the least
affronted to think how little she had helped her in her own
misery, she welcomed her joyfully, and gave her the best seat,
and put before her the best things she had to eat in the house;
whereas the other, when she went, had only received her in the
kitchen, and never asked her to sit down!

After some time, she said, "Sister, pray tell me, where has
your husband found work, that my husband may try and find
some too, for we have fallen into great distress."

And the poor woman answered her, "My husband has not got
any employment, but the day you made me wash my hands he
went away ——" and then she told her all that had happened.

Then the rich woman asked her to take her husband and show
him the dragons. "Perhaps," said she, "we, too, may thus find
succour."

And the poor one said to her, "When my husband comes this
evening I will tell him, and your husband can go to-morrow, with
a bag, along with him."

When the poor man came home at nightfall, his wife told him
what had passed, and he said to her,

"I will go and show him the place, but I will not go to gather
more treasures for myself, for this which I have God blesses, and
it grows from day to day."

Next morning the rich man came with his bag on his back, and
said to him, "Good morrow, brother, how do you do? Are you
well?" Whereas at other times, if he saw his brother in the way
he would turn his back upon him, or take another road, so as not
to hear him say that he wanted any help. But when the poor
man saw him he got up and kissed him, and said, "Welcome,
brother; I daresay it's ten years since I had the happiness of
seeing you enter my house."

"Yes," said the rich one, "but now I have fallen into distress,
and know not what to do."

Says the poor man, "Let us go; perhaps you will have good luck yet, and get as rich as ever." So they set off for the hill.

And when they got there he showed him the tree, and said to him, "Go aloft and sit in the tree, and soon the dragons will come out. Count them. If there are forty-nine you can come down and enter the castle free from fear; but if, peradventure, they are but forty-eight, do not go in." With these words he went away. In a little while the dragons came out, and he began to count them. But it seems he counted them wrong, and instead of saying forty-eight he said forty-nine. So he came down as fast as he could and went into the castle, and eagerly looked about to see where the treasure was, that he might fill his bag and be gone with all speed, and as he stood there he heard a voice saying, "So you are the thief, and have come back to steal more!" And lo! out comes the dragon which had been watching in a room close by, and seizes him by the head and makes four quarters of him, and hangs them up at the four corners of the dwelling. When the dragons came home, he said to them, "There's no need to keep watch any longer, for I have hung up the four quarters of the thief, and they will guard our castle for us!" And from that day forward they determined, none of them to stay at home, but all of them to go out, and so they began to do.

When two days had passed away the wife of the rich man got restless, and went to the house of her brother-in-law to ask him what they had done with her husband. But the poor man told her what directions he had given him, and said, "I don't know whether he has counted the dragons right, but I will go and see." And off he went. When he came near to the castle, he got up into the tree, and when the dragons came out he counted them with great care, and they were forty-nine in all. Then he came down and went into the castle and looked right and left for his brother. And raising his eyes he looked aloft and beheld his brother hanging in four quarters, and he was sore amazed. Then he lost no time in taking him down, filling his bag with money and going away. When he got home he felt very weary and sad, and said to his wife, "Send some one to my sister-in-law's to tell her to come and take charge of her husband."

And when she came she wept, and would not be comforted on beholding her husband cut into four quarters. Then she said to the poor man, "You must find me a tailor to sew him together, for I cannot bury him like that in four pieces."

The poor man went out at once and got a tailor, who sewed him together. When they had buried and bewailed him, the poor man opened the bag and gave his sister-in-law half the money, and said to her, "Go and get succour for yourself and your children, and if you are in want again, do not blush to come and ask me for what you need." The widow went home with tears in her eyes.

Let us leave them and return to the dragons.

When they reached their castle and found the dead man was gone, they all cried aloud, "So the thief has an accomplice!"

The next day, therefore, they went into the town and sought for a tailor to make them forty-nine coats and forty-nine pairs of shoes. So they said to the tailor, "Mind you sew them well so that the stitches don't come out and that they fit us nicely!" And they said it over and over again till the tailor got angry and said to them, "Here's a fuss! why yesterday I had to sew a dead man, who was in four bits, together, and they were quite satisfied with the job, though it was out of my line, and you with your coats are like to craze me!"

Then they said to him, "Pray do you know the man who brought you the dead man to sew?" Said he, "Of course I do, he lives quite close, and if you like I will show you his house, so that you can go and ask him, whether the dead man was well sewed or not."

So he took a dragon with him, and after walking twenty good paces, he showed them the shop. Then they went away to a joiner's, and ordered forty-eight chests, just big enough for them to get into. When they were finished, the forty-eight dragons got inside, and the forty-ninth remained outside. And in the morning the dragon went to the poor man's place, and said to him, "I have had forty-eight chests sent me and I want you to be so kind as to let me leave them here for the night."

"Not for one night only," he answered, "but let them stay as long as you like, and until it suits you to take them away." And he got porters to bring them in.

Then the children of the poor man began to get upon the chests, and jump about, and play on them; and the dragons who were inside, from time to time, groaned and said, " Ah, would it were dark that we might eat them all."

One of the children was playing hide-and-seek with the rest, and he heard these words and these groanings. So he ran to his father and said : " Those chests are bewitched; they are talking."

Then the father thought a moment, and said, " Forty-eight ! and the one that brought them makes forty-nine." And he went close up to the chests, and put his ear at the key-hole, and he, too, heard the groaning. So he said to himself, "Now, monsters, I'll make sure of you, now that I have got you in my power."

So off he set at once, and went and bought forty-eight spits, and lighted his kitchen fire, and put them in, and made them red hot, and took them one by one, and thrust them into all the chests. Then he said to his servant, " Look here, my man, they have played us a trick, and put a dragon in a chest, and if we had not killed it, it would have eaten us all up." The servant was angry, and said to his master, "Give it me, and let me go sink it by the sea shore? " And he took it on his back, and threw it on to the beach. While he was on his way back, his master made ready another one, and said, " You did not throw it far enough out to sea, and it has come back." And as often as he returned he did the same with all, and threw them into the sea.

But when he got to the last one he grew tired of always coming back and finding one there again, so he walked right into the sea, and plunged it in deep, and when he got back to the shop he called out :

" Master, is it back again ? " And his master answered, " No, no, it has not come back. You must have thrown it in very deep." " Aye, master," said he, "I went right into the sea, and plunged it in, and left it."

In the morning the dragon came to see what had become of the chests, and the merchant cunningly told him that one chest was found open, "and I don't know," says he, "what you had inside." He was seized with fear, and went to look at the chests, which were in the back part of the shop. And he found the chest was indeed open, and he trembled. The merchant lost no time, but seized him and flung him into the chest, and made it fast forthwith, and straightway spitted him, and so they were all done for. And the man himself inherited the dragon's castle, and lived there as happy as a prince, and may we live happier still.

———————

THE NINE DOVES.

(THERA.)

---:0:---

ONCE upon a time there was a king who had an only daughter. So he built a tower of glass and put her into it. Her food was nothing but lean meat without any bone in it. One day she says to him, " Pray is all meat the same as I eat ? " Says he, " No, there is bone as well." Says she, " Bring me some like what you eat." They bring it her, she eats it, and flings the bone at the flag. It smashes the glass, and makes a little window.

Then she began to sit by the window, and bask in the sunshine that then chanced to be coming through.

There were passing at the moment nine doves, eight black, and one white. The white dove leaves the rest and comes in at the window. She lifts her hand to catch it, and drops her ring. The white dove takes it in its beak, and flies off with it. Some days afterwards the same bird comes back. As she moves her arm, she drops her bracelet, and the bird flies away with it.

After the same length of time had passed it comes back again. She chases it with her handkerchief ; it catches it and flies off with it. Now she began to cry, to think that her father, who had shut her up, would find them missing. Then she begged her father to build her a cloister in the country, and everyone that passed, she took him in, and asked what he had seen, what he knew, hoping thus to learn if anyone had found her things, and could give them back to her. Now let us leave her, and come to an old woman who had one son, who was half-witted : and he found the secret out. Says he, " Mother dear, I am going to the Queen, so wash me."

" What are you thinking of, my lad ? Do nothing of the sort, for the Queen will not receive such a poor fellow as you."

Says he, " Go, I will."

Since she could not content him, she said to him, "Come, get me wood to make a fire, that I may wash your shirt, that you may go a bit clean, at any rate." So he took his axe and his little donkey, and went out. On his way, when he had tied his donkey to the stump of a tree, just as he was going to fetch a blow with his axe to cut a great log, up comes a donkey going the other way.

"Oh, my donkey!" he cries, and leaves his axe and runs to catch it. As the two went along one after the other, the donkey comes to a stand before a black door, and it opened and they went in, and it shut behind them. As they went on they saw a high staircase, up which the donkey went with the boy after him. Going upstairs into a room, he loses sight of the donkey, and is left alone. There he saw a cauldron boiling. He removes it and sees two partridges. He takes one and leaves the other. He sees a cupboard and gets inside it, and there he ate the partridge. As he sat there, he looked out of the chink, and about mid-day came nine doves. They entered the house, shook themselves, and eight of them became dragons, but the white one remained in the chamber where the old dame's son was, shook itself, and turned into a young man, who claps his hands, and in comes a maid with a basin and towel, and he washes himself.

When he was washed, she placed a table before him, and said, " Master, there were two partridges, I have only found one."

" Never mind," says he, " serve it up; it does not matter."

He ate, the table was cleared, and he was left alone.

He spread out a handkerchief upon the table, and took out the bracelet and the ring, and put them on it, and kissed them, and wept, saying :

" Oh, Princess, since I took your handkerchief, I see you no more in your chamber when I pass." So speaking, he kissed them.

Then, in the midst of his grief, the dragons come, they take him with them, and nine doves fly away.

The lad in terror came out of the cupboard as soon as the dragons had gone, in order to run away. The donkey stands before him. He goes down the stairs, the black door opens ; they go towards the place where his faggots were lying. The donkey disappears, he turns round and sees his own donkey tied to the tree. " Oh, my darling little donkey," says he, " I tied you up, and you got loose by yourself, and tied yourself up again, all to save me trouble."

He took his axe, chopped the wood, and went home to his mother. She lights a fire, washes his shirt, dries it, and puts it on him.

Then he runs, and goes to the Princess, and tells her everything. As soon as she hears it, a great longing seizes her to go.

" Ah," says he, " are you to take your ease, while I go mad with trouble, who am my mother's only boy?"

And he spoke right earnestly, and kept bawling it into her ears.

" Then," says she, " take me !"

Says he, " I won't take you."

But by dint of money and promises he consents to take her, and sets off with her. And he takes a sprig of pepper with him.

Says he, " If you chance to stumble and fall on the ground, or do anything of that sort with me, I will stuff this pepper in your mouth."

The Princess only laughed, and hurried him on. He brought her to the place, put her in the cupboard, and she saw everything. She could not refrain herself, but came out and embraced the youth. Then the boy ran away, and went to the cloister with his mother, and she lived with him there. The Princess lived with the youth eight or nine months. He used to hide her, and go out with the dragons. Then he said to her, " Go to a place which I will tell you of, where I have a sister, until your child is born, and then I will come to you." In course of time a son was born to her, and when he was six weeks old she said to her sister-in-law :

" Sister-in-law, I should like to build a glass palace somewhere in the country, where we could stay, and have it fenced outside with iron."

So when they had made the palace, and the two girls had gone into it, the doves passed by, and as they passed the white one came inside. And they locked the others out with the iron gate.

From their grief at having lost their son, the dragons swelled up and burst with a bang. But lo and behold, the white dove had three pins on the top of its head, and did not remember to tell the Princess to take them out. Then the dove fell on to the bed and began to pant and gasp for its life, because it could not manage to turn into a man.

She put the child upon him, and said, " Let us all three go near him, for he is dying." The babe tumbled over him, and pulled out the pins, when he became a Prince. " Ah, my beloved Princess," says he, " had I been left as I was but another hour, we should both of us have been lost."

Then he took her and his sister and brought them to his father and they lived happily.

MY LADY SEA.

(THERA.)

———:o:———

THERE was once an old man who had his house upon the sand. He was a shoemaker by trade. Now his house was small and had one little window and one door. Moreover the old man was all alone. One day he got tired of this, so he went and got some meal, kneaded it into a great lump of dough, and made it into three pieces. Then he moulded it into three dolls like fair maidens. Then he took and dressed them ; the one in red, the other in blue, and the third in white. He had also a pot with a plant of rosemary in it. In the morning before he went out the old man, who was proud of his daughters, took the one with the white dress, and set her at the window, and put the pot of rosemary by her, and said to her, " My lass, lest you should feel lonely now that I am going away, you can sit at the window and amuse yourself by looking at the people passing. Mind you behave yourself, and make no acquaintances."

The old man locks the door with the key, and goes away to his work. Thereupon as the people pass, on their walks, there comes by among the rest the king's son, who sees the maiden at the window and stops. He bids her good day, and says to her, " Ah, how I love you ! would that you loved me too, and I would make you a queen." He beseeches her to speak with him, but she says not a word, so he cuts off a sprig of rosemary, throws some coins into the lap of the maiden, and makes off to the palace. At nightfall the old man comes home, sees the rosemary gone, and the coins in her lap, seizes her hand and flings her on the floor. " You graceless disgusting creature," he exclaims. " Why, I've never let you go outside the house, and you've got into mischief already ! "

He cuts her up into pieces, opens a cupboard, puts her in,

picks up the money, shuts the window, and goes to sleep. Next
morning he gets up and puts the other with the blue dress at the
window, and says to her, "See that *you* behave yourself," locks
her in and goes away. And lo and behold, the Prince came by
again, quite desperately in love, and said to her, "My darling,
my life! yesterday you were dressed in white, and to-day you are
in blue. Won't you speak to me, when I want to take you to
the palace, and make a queen of you; but will you drive me
mad?" Then he besought her earnestly, but as she did not
speak, he cut another sprig of rosemary, and flung coins to her,
and fled. The old man comes home, and what should he see but
the rosemary clipped, and the coins. "Why," says he, "you are
madder than your sister!" So he takes her by the ear and pulls
her down, and chops her up and puts her in the cupboard; takes
care of the money, and shuts the window fast.

Next morning he set up the third, with the red dress, warned
her well, and went his way. The Prince, as usual, rises, goes out
walking, sees her, and is like to lose his wits. Says he, "My
darling, my life! the day before yesterday you were in white,
yesterday in blue, and to-day in red, and all to send me mad!
Speak to me, my darling; speak to me, my sweet! Have you no
pity on me, my father's only son? Speak to me, and let me take
you to the palace and make a queen of you." But as she did
not speak, he clips off a sprig of rosemary, flings her money, and
goes away sadly to the palace. The old man comes and finds it
the same with her, takes her and pulls her down, and chops her
up, and puts her in the cupboard, and says, "There you are,
since you've all of you determined I am not to have you as
daughters, but have so disgraced yourselves." So he shut the
window and opened it no more.

For three mornings the Prince passed, as was his wont, and
sees the window closed, and falls ill with grief.

The King comes, the doctors come, medicine comes for the
Prince, but he gets worse instead of better. The doctors say to
the King, "Beg him, Oh King, to tell you what ails him, for this is
no common sickness." "Father," says he, "what shall I tell you?
I saw a fair maiden at such and such a window, and if I may not
win her, I shall die."

"Well, my son, we must see where she is."

Messengers are sent to seek her. They make inquiries and are told, "An old man lives in that house." After hunting in all directions they find him. Says the messenger, "You must come, the King wants you." The poor fellow was seized with great fear. Says he, "What does the King want with me?" He goes to the palace, and the King says to him, "Old man, you must bring me your daughter." The old man was afraid to tell him he had not got one. Said the King, "Bring me your daughter, or I shall kill you. Come, old man," he continued, "you'd better bring her, you know what will happen if you don't."

Then the old man left. Says he, "There's nothing for it but to seek among my acquaintance for some girl to bring him."

He went into the wood. There an old woman met him and said to him, "Eh, old man, whither away?" Says he, "Let me alone, will you? for I am going to dash my brains out over a precipice." Says she, "Nay, but you must tell me." Says he, "The King wants my daughter, and I have no daughter."

"Old man," said she, "take this whip and go to the shore, and strike it upon the sea, and call three times 'My Lady Sea,' Come calm, come storm, raise no alarm!" So he went to the shore and struck upon the sea with the whip. A gentle wave came up. He cried, "Oh, Lady Sea, what think you? The King sends word that you should send him your daughter, that he may give her in marriage."

"If he will wait three days and three nights," was the answer, "that I may array her, I will send her."

So the old man waited, and sent word up to the King that in six days he would bring him his daughter. When the King heard it, he sent down to the old man a guard, and every comfort, and bade them give him bed and board. In three days and three nights the sea retreated and left the shore dry, and there came out a maiden, at the brightness of whose beauty he was thunderstruck. Then the old man takes her as his daughter, along with the soldiers who were guarding him, and goes up to the palace. And for garments her mother dressed her with the sky and the stars, with the field and the flowers, with the sea and the ships that sail thereon; the countless pebbles of the sand she put on her for pearls; of the little shells upon the shore she made her rings for her fingers, and the raven's wing she gave her for an arching eyebrow. Then he took her to the palace, and when the Prince saw her, he set her in the best chamber, and paid her every attention, and spoke to her, but she would not speak to him. Then he besought her day and night upon his bended knee: "My darling! you would not believe me then, when you were at the window "—for he thought she was the one he had seen at the window—"when I said I would take you for my bride; but won't you believe me now that I am ready to wed you?" He weeps, he despairs, night and day, entreating her to speak to him, but speak to him she would not. Once on a time, when the Prince had gone out to divert his grief, she told her maid to get her ready a stove of coals, and a frying-pan filled with oil. They put it on the stove, and it began to boil before her, and then she put in her hands when it had boiled and bubbled, and the frying-pan was filled with such barbel as were a dish fit for the King. When they were fried she put them by, and in the evening she set them on the King's table. Says he, "Who did those fish?" They say, "The old man's daughter;" and he was pleased.

Then the next day the Prince went to her and entreated her, but as she would not speak to him, he was much troubled, and went to sleep on a couch in the same room, that he might recover from the grief which dazed him. By his pillow there was a window, and she took and made two little dolls as big as one of our fingers, in full dress, and put them at the window, when they began to quarrel with one another, and one of them said, "Where are my shoes, and where is my handkerchief?" and the other, "Where is my petticoat? Give me my petticoat!" And they raised their voices so loud that the Prince opened his eyes and saw the two dolls at the window quarrelling. And when they saw him they ceased their noise; but the one said to the other—

"Just look at the Prince! what a fool he is!"

"Why?" said the other.

"Why, he has had our mistress all this time, and he can't make her speak!"

"And what ought he to say to her?"

" He should say to her, ' I wish you joy of your Sire the Sun, and of your Mother the Lady Sea.' " And all at once the dolls vanished from the window without his seeing whither they went— for they were barbels out of the sea, and the maiden had changed them into dolls.

The Prince's curiosity was roused.

But when he saw them no more, he got up and went to the Princess and begged her again to speak to him. " For," said he, " in the course of conversation I will bring in the saying that I heard from the dolls." For it seemed to him like a dream.

Then just when he came to the words, "I wish you joy of your Sire the Sun, and of your Mother the Lady Sea," she spoke to him, and threw her arms round his neck. And at once the wedding was made ready, and they were married and lived a right merry life together.

LITTLE SADDLESLUT.

[THE GREEK CINDERELLA.]

(EPIRUS.)

—— :0: ——

THERE were once three sisters spinning flax, and they said, "Whosever spindle falls, let us kill her and eat her."

The mother's spindle fell, and they left her alone.

Again they sat down to spin, and again the mother's spindle fell, and again and yet again. "Ah, well!" said they, "let us eat her now!"

"No!" said the youngest, "do not eat her; eat me, if flesh you will have."

But they would not; and two of them killed their mother and cooked her for eating.

When they had sat down to make a meal of her, they said to the youngest, "Come and eat too!"

But she refused, and sat down on a saddle which the fowls were covering with filth, and wept, and upbraided them. Many a time they said to her, "Come and eat!" but she would not; and when they had done eating, they all went away. Then the youngest, whom they called Little Saddleslut, gathered all the bones together and buried them underneath the grate, and smoked them every day with incense for forty days; and after the forty days were out, she went to take them away and put them in another place. And when she lifted up the stone, she was astonished at the rays of light which it sent forth, and raiment was found there, like unto the heavens and the stars, the spring with its flowers, the sea with its waves; and many coins of every kind; and she left them where she found them. Afterwards her sisters came and found her sitting on the saddle, and jeered at her. On Sunday her sisters went to church; then she, too, arose; she washed and attired herself, putting on the garment that was as the heavens with the stars, and went to church, taking with her a few gold pieces in her purse. When she went into the church all the people were amazed, and could not gaze upon her by reason of the brightness of her garments. When she left the church, the people followed her to see whither she went. Then she filled her hand with money from her bag and cast it in the way, and so she kept throwing it down all the way she went, so that they might not get near her. Then the crowd scrambled for the coins, and left her alone. And straightway she went into her house, and changed her clothes, and put on her old things, and sat down upon the saddle. Her sisters came home from church and said to her, "Where are you, Wretch? Come and let us tell you how there came into the church a maiden more glorious than the sun, who had such garments on as you could not look on, so brightly did they gleam and shine, and she strewed money on the way! Look, see what a lot we have picked up! Why did not you come too? worse luck to you!"

. "You are welcome to what you picked up; I don't want it," said she.

Next Sunday they went to church again, and she did the same. Then they went another Sunday, and just as she was flinging the money, she lost her shoe among the crowd, and left it behind her. Now the King's son was following her, but could not catch her, and only found her shoe. Then said he to himself, "Whose ever foot this shoe exactly fits, without being either too large or too small, I will take her for my wife." And he went to all the women he knew and tried it on, but could not manage to fit it. Then her sisters came to her and spoke as follows to her, "You go and try; perhaps it will fit you!"

"Get away with you!" said she. "Do you think he will put the shoe on me, and get it covered with filth? Do not make fun of me." The Prince had taken all the houses in turn, and so he came at length to the house of Little Saddleslut, and his servants told her to come and try on the shoe.

"Do not make fun of me," she says. However she went down, and when the Prince saw her, he knew the shoe was hers, and said to her, "Do you try on the shoe." And with the greatest ease she put it on, and it fitted her.

Then said the Prince to her, "I will take you to wife."

"Do not make fun of me," she answered, "so may your youth be happy!"

"Nay, but I will marry you," said he, and he took her and made her his wife. Then she put on her fairest robes. When a little child was born to her, the sisters came to see it. And when she was helpless and alone they took her and put her into a chest, and carried her off and threw her into a river, and the river cast her forth upon a desert.

There was a half-witted old woman there, and when she saw the chest, she thought to cut it up [for firewood] and took it away for that purpose. And when she had broken it open, and saw someone alive in it, she got up and made off. So the Princess was left alone, and heard the wolves howling, and the swine and the lions, and she sat and wept and prayed to God, "Oh God, give me a little hole in the ground that I may hide my head in it, and not hear the wild beasts," and He gave her one. Again she said, "Oh God, give me one a little larger, that I may get in up to my waist." And He gave her one. And she besought Him again a third time, and He gave her a cabin with all that she wanted in it: and there she dwelt, and whatever she said, her bidding was done forthwith. For instance, when she wanted to eat, she would say, "Come, table with all that is wanted! Come food! Come spoons and forks, and all things needful," and straightway they all got ready, and when she finished she would ask, "Are you all there?" and they would answer, "We are."

One day the Prince came into the wilderness to hunt, and seeing the cabin he went to find out who was inside; and when he got there he knocked at the door. And she saw him and knew him from afar, and said, "Who is knocking at the door?" "It is I, let me in," said he. "Open, doors!" said she, and in a twinkling the doors opened and he entered. He went upstairs and found her seated on a chair. "Good day to you," said he, "Welcome!" said she, and straightway all that was in the room cried out, "Welcome!" "Come chair!" she cried, and one came at once. "Sit down," she said to him and down he sat.

And when she had asked him the reason of his coming, she bade him stay and dine, and afterwards depart.

He agreed, and straightway she gave her orders : "Come table with all the covers," and forthwith they presented themselves, and he was sore amazed. "Come basin," she cried. "Come jug, pour water for us to wash ! Come food in ten courses !" and immediately all that she ordered made its appearance. Afterwards when the meal was ended, the Prince tried to hide a spoon, and put it into his shoe ; and when they rose from table, she said "Table, have you all your covers ?"

"Yes I have."

"Spoons, are you all there ?"

"All," they said, except one which said "I am in the Prince's shoe."

Then she cried again, as though she had not heard, "Are you all there, spoons and forks ?"

And as soon as the Prince heard her he got rid of it on the sly and blushed.

And she said to him "Why did you blush ? Don't be afraid. I am your wife."

Then she told him how she got there and how she fared. And they hugged and kissed each other, and she ordered the house to move and it did move. And when they came near the town all the world came out to see them. Then the Prince gave orders for his wife's sisters to be brought before him, and they brought them and he hewed them in pieces. And so henceforward they lived happily, and may we live more happily still.

STARBRIGHT AND BIRDIE.

(EPIRUS.)

———:0:———

I WILL begin my tale, by wishing your worships good evening.

Once upon a time there was a woman who had two children. the one a boy whom they called Starbright, and the other a girl whom they called Birdie. One day the husband went out hunting, and brought his wife a pigeon and gave it her to cook for dinner. She took the pigeon and hung it on the spit and went out to gossip with the neighbours. Then comes the cat and sees the pigeon hanging on the spit and pounces on it and carries it off and eats it. When dinner time comes, the women get up from their gossip, and the good wife goes to fetch the pigeon, and cannot find it. And she saw that the cat had taken it, and was afraid her husband would scold her, so she chopped off a piece of her breast and cooked it. Her husband came home and said, "Well, wife, have you cooked us anything for dinner?"

"I have," she said, and she laid the cloth, and brought the meat for him to eat.

"Sit down, wife, and let's eat," says he.

"I have had my own dinner," said she, "because you were so late in coming."

When the man had swallowed a few mouthfuls he said, "What good meat this is; I never ate such in my life."

Then his wife said to him, "Hear what has happened to me. I had hung the pigeon on the spit, and I went to fetch wood, and came back and could not find it. The cat had taken it. What was I to do? I cut a piece off my breast and cooked it, and if you don't believe me, look!" and she showed him the wound.

"How nice is human flesh, wife!" cried he. "Do you know

what we'll do? Let's kill and eat our children. To-morrow morning we will go to church and you shall go home first, and kill them, and cook them, and then I will come too, and we'll eat them." Now there was a little dog there that heard what they were saying. And while the children were asleep, the dog came and barked "Yap! Yap!" and a voice was heard saying, "Get up, your mother is coming to kill you." "Tut! Tut!" said they. But the dog went on again in the same strain. Then when they heard plainly, they got up in haste, and made ready to fly. "What shall we take with us, Birdie dear?" says the boy.

"I don't know, my Starbright," says the girl. "Take a knife, and a comb, and a handful of salt." They took them, and went off, not knowing whither, taking the dog with them, and as they were going along, lo and behold! there they saw their mother, a long way off, running after them. Starbright turned round and says, "Look! Mother is after us; she will catch us up."

"Go on, darling," says the maiden, "and she won't catch us."

"She is up to us, Birdie dear, look!" says the boy.

"Throw down your knife behind you," says she; and he threw it down and it became a field which had no bound. But the mother ran so fast that she caught them up again.

"She is up with us," says the boy again.

"Go on," says she, "and they won't overtake us."

"But they have overtaken us," said he again, "Quick, throw away your comb," said she. He threw the comb and it became a thick forest. She passed over that also, and the third time they threw down the salt, and it became a sea and the parents could not cross over it. Then the girl stood still and looked across and her mother said to her, "Come back, my darling, and I won't do you any harm." But they would not. She threatened them and beat her breast in her rage.

But they still would not listen to her, and began to go further. And when they had gone a long way, Starbright said, "Birdie, I am thirsty." "Go on," said she, "yonder is the King's fountain, and you can drink." When they had gone some way further, the boy said again, "I am thirsty; I shall die." And just there they found a hole made by a wolf's hoof, with water in it, and he said to her, "I will drink here." "Don't drink," said she, "or you will turn into a wolf and eat me." "If so, I won't drink," said he, and they went on again. They go on and on till they find a hole made by a sheep's hoof with water in it. "I'll drink here, I can stand it no longer; I'm done for."

"Don't drink," says Birdie to him, "or you will be turned into a lamb, and they will kill you."

"Let them kill me," said he, "but drink I will."

So he drank, and became a lamb, and ran after her bleating : "Baa, Birdie, Baa, Birdie."

"Come along with me," said Birdie, and they went on a little and found the King's fountain, and drank water. Then said Birdie to the lamb, "Sit down here with the dog, my darling," and she went and prayed to God underneath a tall, tall cypress tree and said, "Oh God, give me strength to get up into the top of this cypress, and grant my prayer." And strength from on high lifted her up to the top of the cypress, and there, where she sat, appeared a golden throne, and the lamb stayed down below beside the dog underneath the cypress, and grazed. In a little while the King's servants came to water their horses, and when they got close to the cypress the horses took fright and broke their traces and fled before the brightness of Birdie, who was very fair, and shone from the top of the cypress.

"Come down !" said the servants to her, "the horses are afraid to drink water."

"I won't come down," says she, "let the horses drink water; I will do them no harm."

"Come down," say they again to her.

"I won't come down," says she.

Then they go to the Prince and tell him, as follows :—"By the fountain, up in a cypress, there sits a maiden, the brightness of whose beauty is such that the horses are afraid of its sheen, and will not drink; and we told her to come down and she won't." When the Prince heard that he arose and came to the place and told her himself to come down, and she would not. A second and a third time he said, "Come down ; we will fell the tree if you do not come down." "Fell it," says she, "I sha'n't come down." So they got men to fell the tree, and while they were hacking at it, the lamb went and licked the tree, and it got twice as thick as it was before. They hewed and hewed, to cut it down ; but in vain.

"Get away with you all," said the Prince, in his wrath, and away they ran. He then goes in his grief to an old woman, and says to her, "If you will fetch me that girl down from the cypress, I will fill your bonnet with money."

"I'll fetch her down for you," says the old woman ; and she takes a trough and sieve and some flour and goes to the foot of the cypress tree and turns the trough and the sieve upside down, and so begins to sift. The girl then looks down from the cypress and calls out, "Turn the trough the other way, good mother, and turn the sieve the other way, too!"

The "good mother" on her part made believe not to hear, and said, "Eh, my darling, who are you? Can't hear you."

"The other way up with the sieve ; the other way up with the trough!" said she for the second and the third time. The "good mother" answered her again, "I can't hear you, my darling! who are you? I don't see you. Come and show me, and may God bless you!" And so the maiden little by little came down, and just when she was going to show her, out came the Prince who had been hiding there and seized her, and led her off, and the lamb and the dog followed behind. And when they came to the royal palace, he made a feast and took her for his wife. The King loved his daughter-in-law very much, but the Queen was jealous of her. One day when the Prince went out the Queen called her maid-servants and told them to take her daughter-in-law a walk in the garden, and throw her into the well. The maid-servants did as the Queen bade them, and threw her into the well. Afterwards, when the Prince came home and could not see her, he asked his mother : "Mother, where is the bride?"

"Gone out," said she, "to take a walk ; and it might be as well," she added, "now that she is not here, to slay the lamb." "True!" said the rest. The lamb heard this and ran to the well, and said to Birdie, "Birdie dear, they are going to kill me."

"Hush, my darling!" said she. "They sha'n't kill you."

"Only look! they are sharpening the knives! they have caught me! they will kill me!"

"What can I do for you, my darling? do you not see where I am?"

Then the maid-servants caught the lamb, and were about to kill it, and just as they were lifting the knife against it, Birdie prayed to God, and said, "Oh God, they are killing my brother, and here am I in the well!" In a twinkling she had leapt from the well and went and found the lamb, whose throat they had cut. She screams and calls to them to let it go. But they had cut its throat. "Oh, my lamb!" she screams and cries, "Oh, my lamb, my lamb!" She will not be comforted. The King comes and says, "What do you want, my precious one? Tell me what you want and I will give it you."

"Nothing," says she, "my lamb, my lamb!"

"What's done can't be undone," says he, "only be quiet."

And when they had cooked it, they served it up for dinner. "Come let us eat," they said.

"I have eaten," says she, "I shall eat no more at present."

"Come, my dear, eat," they say again.

"Do you eat," says she, "I have eaten."

When they had finished their meal, she went and gathered all the bones together, and put them in a jar and buried them in the garden. And in the spot where she buried them, there grew up a tall, tall apple tree, and bore a golden apple; and many tried to reach it and could not, for the nearer they got to it, the higher grew the apple-tree. Only when Birdie drew near, it came down again. And Birdie said to the King, "All have been to try, and could not reach the apple, let me go too; perhaps I shall reach it."

"What?" says he, "when so many tall people have tried and have not been able to reach it, do you think you can do so?"

"Let me go too," said she, "do me the favour."

"Well, then, you can go," said he to her.

And no sooner did she approach than the apple-tree grew lower, and Birdie reached the apple; and the apple said to her, "Draw me gently, gently, so as not to bruise me."

And she took it and put it in her pocket, and cried, "Farewell, my dearest father-in-law ; and as for that cruel mother-in-law of mine, may she sleep and never wake ! " And she fled and returned no more. And God took pity upon her and she became the constellation of the Dove (Pleiades) and Starbright —the evening star.

THE GOLDEN WAND.

(EPIRUS.)

———:∩:———

THERE was a merchant who traded in the Indies and who had three daughters. Once when he set off on his journey to the Indies his daughters besought him as follows : the first to bring her an Indian dress, the second an Indian turban, and the third the Golden Wand. And they adjured him by a spell so that if he did not bring the things, his ship should not leave the shore. When he got to the Indies he obtained all the merchandise he desired, and also what two of his daughters had begged of him, only he forgot to get the Golden Wand for his youngest daughter. When, then, he prepared to leave the Indies, although it was fair weather, his ship would not leave the shore. Then he sat down and considered, and a countryman passed by and asked why he was so thoughtful. The merchant did not wish to tell him. Then the countryman entreated him to do so, and said to him, " Think : have you not made some promise ? "

The merchant thought and remembered what he had promised his youngest daughter, and asked the countryman where the Golden Wand was to be found. Then the countryman pointed to a road and said to him, that he must walk for three hours and he would come upon the Golden Wand. And the merchant did as the countryman told him, and walked for three hours, and came to a place and asked there, " Where is the Golden Wand ? " And they showed him a palace, and told him that inside it was the Golden Wand, and that it was the name of the King's son. He was afraid when they told him it was the King's son, but afterwards he plucked up heart and went to the palace and asked leave from the King to enter, and the King gave him leave. And when the King asked him what he wanted, he told him that he wished to speak with the Prince. The King led him

into the room where the Prince was sitting, and the Prince asked
him, " What do you want with me ? " And the merchant told
him all that his daughter had said to him. Then the Prince took
him into a room where there were pictures of a number of
maidens and asked him :

" Is your daughter as fair as these ? "

And he said to him : " Oh, a thousand times fairer ! "

Then he took him into another room where there was a picture
of one whom he had seen in his sleep and dreamt he was to
take to wife ; and he asked him :

" Is your girl as fair as that ? "

And he answered : " Why it is she herself ! "

Then the Prince gave him a letter, and a cup, and a ring to
give to his daughter. And the merchant took them on board
his ship. And forthwith the ship left the shore and sailed away
home. When he came to his home, his daughters asked him,
" Well, father, have you brought us the things you promised
us ? "

" I have," said he, and he took them out and gave each one
what he had promised her. He gave also to the youngest the
letter, the cup, and the ring which the Prince had given him.
And she took them and went and shut herself up alone in her
room, and opened the letter and read it and saw what he wrote
to her, which was, that when she wanted him she was to put
water in the cup and then to put the ring into the water and to
say three times, " Come, come, come, my Golden Wand ! " and
that he himself would come in the shape of a dove, and would
wash in the water, and become a man : and she was to leave an
opening in the ceiling for him to come in by.

Then she did as he wrote to her, and the dove came, and after
swimming in the water it turned into a man ; and when they had
talked for a long time together, it again took a swim in the
water and became a dove and flew away. As it flew it left her
a cactus-berry behind, and told her to break it open, and to put
on what she found inside.

When he was gone she opened it and found within it a fine
dress on which were embroidered the heavens and the stars.
She put it on and went out. When her sisters saw it they

wondered and began to ask her questions, and grew jealous of her. She did the same thing another time, and again Golden Wand came, and when he went away he left her a nut, and told her to break it and put on what she found inside. And when the dove was gone, then she broke open the nut and found a dress which had a picture on it of the sea with the waves, and she put it on and went out. Again her sisters wondered as they saw her and were more jealous of her than ever. Again she put the cup full of water before her, and said thrice, "Come, come, come, my Golden Wand!" And he came and swam in the water and became a man. When he went away again, he left her a fig, and told her to cut it open, and put on what she found inside. When he was gone, she cut it open and inside she found another dress whereon was a picture of May, with all its flowers. She put it on and went out.

Then the sisters wondered more than ever and took counsel together how they might work her woe, and said to one another that when they went to bathe, the eldest should take a bag of pearls, and make believe to spill them, and stay behind the rest to pick them up; and while the others went on to bathe, she, under the pretence of picking up the pearls, should go home and do the same as the youngest used to do—for they had watched her and seen what she did—and make herself out to be the youngest, so that he might give her something too. And in the morning when they went to bathe, the eldest took the bag of pearls, and while they were walking along the road, she made believe to slip, and spilt the pearls and said to the others, " Go on in front while I pick up my pearls," and when the others had gone on some distance she swept them all up in a moment, and put them in her bag and went home, and took the key of the youngest one's chamber, and went in (for she had watched where she put the key), and she opened the cupboard and took the cup and filled it with water and put in the ring.

But her youngest sister had a knife and she had forgotten it and left it on the cup, and when the other said, "Come, my Golden Wand!" the Prince came and swam, and when he was about to rise he cut himself against the knife, and got up and fled. When she saw the blood in the water, she was much distressed. She left the cup with the blood in it in the cupboard, and ran away to join the other girls. And when they returned the youngest went into her room, and on entering she said, " Come, my Golden Wand, and see me, now that I have been and bathed." And when she went to take the cup, she sees it full of blood. She weeps and wails and cries, " Alas ! what has befallen me ? " and after weeping much she went out. But she saw what her sisters had done, and she went to her father and said to him :

" Sire, cut me out a fine dress in the Frankish fashion and give me a good ship that I may go abroad."

Then her father cut her out the Frankish dress, and she put it on, and went on board the ship to sail for the Indies to find him. And as she went in the way she saw a bird who was overtaking another, and the first bird, who, by-the-bye, was a dove, said to him, " Are you not grieved that the Prince is ill, and that the doctors have given him up ? "

And the other bird said to him, " The doctors don't know it ; but the Prince may yet be healed."

The other bird asked him, " With what medicine may he be healed ? "

And his companion answered him, " They must kill us, and take us and a little water from that spring over there, and make an ointment and anoint his throat where he is wounded, and he will be healed."

The maiden, when she heard these words (for she knew the language of doves from Golden Wand), understood what the birds said. Then she fired a gun and killed both of them, and took them, and a little water from the spring they spoke of, and made the ointment and went to the seraglio of the Prince and stood below and cried, " A good physician, a good physician ! and good physic too ! " Then the King heard her and called out from overhead, and said to her, " Can you heal my son ? " And she said to him, " Let me see him." And when she saw him she said to the King, "In eight days' time I will have him healed and send him out to hunt."

When the King heard that he was glad.

The other doctors who heard him say how he was going to

heal him, said, "If he heals your son as he says, you may cut off our heads."

Then the "Doctor" went to the Prince and anointed him with the ointment, and he got better; and after two days he began to speak. And when she had applied the ointment many times, in eight days she had healed him and sent him out to hunt.

When his father saw him he was very pleased and said to the "Doctor," "What good thing do you wish me to do to you for the good you have done to me?"

And the "Doctor" said, "I wish for nothing else from your Majesty except that you should make a feast for me, and call to it all the rulers of India."

Then the King said to him, "What you ask for is nothing to me." And he began to make ready for the feast, and called all the rulers of India, and gave a very great banquet. And when they had eaten and drunk, the "Doctor" said to the King, "Bid them be still, for I have a tale to tell."

Then the King commanded silence, and they were all still, and the "Doctor" began to tell his tale—word by word, as we know it. He told all that had befallen him without saying who he was.

And when he told how the maiden had turned doctor, he declared himself, and said, "I am that maiden and the bride of the Prince, and it was not I that wounded him to death but my sister."

Then when the Prince heard that he embraced her, and said to her, "You are my bride," and they had a splendid wedding and became man and wife.

THE SNAKE, THE DOG, AND THE CAT.

(EPIRUS.)

————:o:————

THERE was a poor woman who had one son, and they had no bread to eat. So the lad took a load of oleander and went and sold it for a couple of coppers. And as he was coming back he found some boys, who were about to kill a snake, and said to them, "There's a copper for you; don't kill it." So he gave them the copper, and the boys did not kill it, and the snake followed him.

When he came home he told his mother what he had done.

And his mother scolded him, and said, "I send you to get money that we may have something to eat, and you bring me snakes!"

And he said, "Never mind, mother; even this will be of some use to us."

Again the lad took some oleander and sold it; and as he came back he saw some boys who were going to kill a dog, and said to them, "There's a copper for you; don't kill it." The boys took the copper and let the dog go. Then it, too, followed him.

The lad went to his mother and told her what he had done. And again his mother scolded him as before.

One more he took some oleander, and sold it, and on his way back he found some boys who were going to kill a cat, and said to them, "Don't kill it, and I will give you a copper." So he gave them the copper and they let the cat go. And when he came home again, he told his mother what he had done, and she scolded him and said to him, "I send you to get money that we may eat bread, and you bring dogs, and cats, and snakes."

Then said he to her, "Never mind, mother; even they will be of some use to us."

Afterwards the snake said to him, " Bring me to my father and mother, and take neither silver nor gold from them, only ask for the signet-ring which my father wears on his finger, and from it you will reap great advantage."

Then he took the snake to its father, and the snake said to its father, "This lad saved me from death."

And the father of the snake said to him, "What shall I give you for the kindness you have shown to my son?"

Then said the lad to the snake's father, "I want neither silver nor gold, I only want the signet-ring which you wear on your finger."

Then said the snake's father to the lad, "It is a great request you make, and more than I can grant."

Then the snake made as though he would follow the boy home, and said to its father, "Since you will not give the signet-ring to him who saved me from death, I will follow him wherever he goes, for to him I owe my life."

Then the father of the snake gave the ring to the boy, and said to him, "Whenever you want anything, press the seal, and there will come a Negro, whom you may bid do whatever you want, and he will do it."

Then the boy left and came to his house. And his mother said to him, "What shall we eat, my darling?" And he said to her, "Go to the cupboard and you will find bread there?"

Then said his mother, "My son, I know there is no bread in the cupboard, and yet you tell me to go and find bread there."

And he said, "Go, as I tell you, and you will find some."

And while she was going to the cupboard he pressed the seal, and the Negro came, and said, "What are your orders, master?" And the lad said to him, "I wish you to fill the cupboard with bread."

And when his mother came to the cupboard she found it full of bread, and took, and ate. In this way they fared well with the signet-ring.

Once on a time the lad said to his mother, "Mother, go to the King and tell him to give me his daughter in marriage." His mother answered him, "What a pass have things come to that the King should give his daughter in marriage to the likes of us!"

But he said, " Go, I tell you."

So the poor woman set off to see the King.

When she was admitted she said to the King, "My son wishes to marry your daughter." Then said the King to her, " I will give her to him if he is able to build a palace larger than mine."

The old woman arose and went to her son, and told him what the King said. And that same night he pressed the seal, and straightway the Negro appeared, and said to him :

" What are your orders, Master ? "

And the other said to him, "That you build a castle larger than that of the King," and forthwith he found himself in a large palace. Then he sent his mother to the King again, and she said to him, " My son has built the castle which you ordered." Said the King to her, " If he is able to pave the street from his palace to mine with gold, then he shall have my daughter in marriage."

Then the old woman went to her son, and told him all these things, and the lad called the Negro, and told him to pave the road all with gold. In the morning the lad got up and found it covered with gold as the King had required. Then his mother went again to the King, and said to him :

"My son has done all that you required." Then the King told her that the wedding should be made ready. And the old woman ran off, and went and told her son what the King had said to her.

The lad then made ready for the wedding.

And the King called his daughter, and told her all that had happened, and that she was to get ready for the marriage.

The daughter was delighted, but begged her father to give her a slave to send whithersoever she would, and her father did as she desired. When the wedding was held, the bridegroom took the bride, and they lived happily for a long time. At length the Princess fell in love with the slave, and one night she stole the signet-ring from her husband and ran away with the slave, and they went to the sea side and built a palace with the seal, and lived together there close to the sea.

When the Princess had gone away with the slave, the cat

came and purred and mewed and said to her master, " Master,
what's the matter ? "

" Matter, indeed ! puss, this is what has befallen me :

" One night, while I was asleep, the slave took my ring and my
wife, and ran away with them."

" Peace, Master," said his cat, " I will go and fetch her.   Give
me the dog to ride, and let me go and fetch the ring."

Then he gives her the dog; and the cat rides him and crosses
the sea.   And as she was going along she found a mouse and said
to it, " If you wish me to spare your life, go and stick your tail
into the slave's nose while he is asleep."   The mouse did so,
and then the slave sneezed, and the ring which he had hidden in
his mouth, fell out of it.   The cat seized it and bestrode the dog,
and while they were swimming in the sea, the dog said to the
cat :

" As you hope to live, puss, stop, and let me just have a peep
at the signet ring."

" Why should you want to look at it, Coz ? "   And as the dog
took the seal, he let it drop into the sea, and a fish snapped it up
and turned all sorts of fine colours.   Then said the cat to the
dog, " Alack, what have you done to me?   How shall I go to my
master without the signet ?   Come along, let's ride you."

And she rode him again till she came where the ships were
drawn ashore.

And in the ship beside which they stopped the captain had
just caught the very fish.   So the cat began to purr and mew
again, till the captain said, " What a nice cat we have here ?
This evening, when I go home and cook the fish, I will throw her
the entrails to eat."   So when he was cleaning the fish and throwing her the entrails, the signet falls out, and the cat seizes it, rides
the dog, and brings it to her master.   And when her master saw
her he said, " Well, puss, have you brought the signet ? "   " I
have," said she, "only you must kill the dog, because he threw it
into the sea, and I have had no end of trouble to find it again,"
and she told him all she had gone through.

Then he took his gun to kill the dog, but now the cat inter-
fered, and said to him, " Spare him this time, because we have
taken our meals together so long "

Then he spared him. After that he took the signet and pressed it, and the Negro comes, and says to him, "What are your orders, Master?"

"That you bring hither the castle that is by the sea," said he.

In a moment the Negro brought it.

The lad went in and found the slave with the Princess, and killed him.

Then he took his wife and they lived happily all their lives.

SIR LAZARUS AND THE DRAGONS.

(EPIRUS.)

————:o:————

THERE was once a cobbler called Lazarus. One day as he was cobbling, a swarm of flies came about him, and he switched a sole at them, and slew forty flies. Then he went and made a sword, and wrote on it, "With one stroke I have taken forty lives." And when he had made his sword, he set off for foreign parts. After two days' journey from his home he came to a spring, and lay down to sleep there. There the dragons were dwelling. Then one came to fetch water, and found Lazarus asleep. He saw also what was written on his sword, and went and told the rest. They told him to go and propose to him that they should become comrades.

The dragon went and called him, and said, "If he liked they would become comrades." Lazarus said he was willing. And they went and lived together.

Then the dragons told him they took it in turn to go for water and also for wood. So the dragons went to fetch wood and water.

At length the turn of Lazarus came to fetch water. The dragons had a skin in which they took the water, and it held two hundred gallons. It was all that Lazarus could do to carry the skin empty to the well, and since he could not carry the water he did not fill the skin, but began digging round the well. The dragons, finding Lazarus was a long time away, were afraid something was wrong, and sent one of their number to go and see what had happened.

The dragon went and said to him, "What are you doing there, Sir Lazarus?"

Says he, "I can't be at the trouble of coming to fetch water every day, so I am going to bring the whole well at once, to save time."

" For God's sake, Sir Lazarus, don't do that," says the dragon, "for we shall die of thirst : we will go in your stead, when it is your turn."

Next it came to the turn of Lazarus to fetch wood ; and as he could not lift a tree like the dragons, he tied all the trees together with thongs. And when it grew late, the dragons again sent one of their number to see what he was doing. "What are you doing there, Sir Lazarus?" said he.

"I am going to bring the whole wood at once, to save trouble," said he.

"Don't do that, Sir Lazarus," says the dragon, "or we shall die of cold : we will go in your stead when it is your turn."

So the dragon took the tree and carried it off.

After some time the dragons thought they would kill him, and they resolved that at nightfall they would all fetch him a stroke with an axe. Lazarus heard what they said, and when evening came he put a log in his bed, and covered it with his cloak. At nightfall they all struck the log at once, and hewed it in pieces, and thought they had killed him. When the dragons had gone to sleep, Lazarus took the log and threw it away, and lay down, and as day began to dawn he murmured something, and the dragons asked him, saying, "What is the matter?"

And he told them that some fleas had been biting him. The dragons supposed that he thought the axe-blows were flea-bites, and next day they told him that if he had wife and children, and thought well, they would give him a supply of money, and let him go home. Lazarus said he was willing, and that he would take one of the dragons with him to carry the money to his house.

While they were on the way, he said to the dragon, "Stop! let me go and tie up my children, lest they eat you."

He went and tied up his children with some old ropes, and said to them, "When you see the dragon, mind you call out 'Dragon's flesh!'"

And when the dragon came near, the children called out, "Dragon's flesh!" The dragon in a great fright left the money and fled.

While he was on his way he met a fox, who asked why he was in such a fright. And he said to him, "That until he had made good his escape, the children of Sir Lazarus were like to eat him." "Are you afraid of Sir Lazarus' children?" said he. "Why he had two hens, one of them I ate yesterday, and the other I am going to eat now. And if you don't believe me, come along with me and see; tie yourself to my tail."

So the dragon tied himself to the fox's tail, and went to see.

When they neared the house of Sir Lazarus, Sir Lazarus was on the look-out with his gun, for he was afraid of the dragons.

When he saw the fox coming along with the dragon, he said to it, "I didn't tell you only to bring that dragon, but to bring them all."

When the dragon heard that, he made off: and from the great force with which he dragged the fox, it died.

So when Sir Lazarus had got rid of the dragons, he did up his house handsomely, and lived at ease.

———————————— ——— . — —

THE LION, THE TIGER, AND THE EAGLE.

(EPIRUS.)

————:o:————

THERE was once a King who had three daughters and three sons. The time came for their father to die, and he said to his sons, "My sons, I am now dying; but do you think to get your sisters married, and afterwards to marry yourselves. As for you," he said to the youngest, "I have a fairy for you shut up in the crystal chamber, and when your sisters are married, see that you get married too." After giving them further counsel, he died. A few days later the Queen died also, and the children were left orphans. A short time passed and there came a lion, and knocked at the door. "Who is there?" cried the King's children. "I am the lion," said he, "come to take your eldest sister to wife."

"How far off is your dwelling?" said they.

"For such as me, five days' journey, and for such as you, five years'," said he.

"Five years!" they cried, "we will not let our sister go. If she should ever fall ill, how could we get to see her?"

But the youngest brother took her by the hand and led her to the lion.

"Go where your fortune takes you," said he. So when they had made love to one another, the lion took her and fled. The next day the tiger came and knocked at the door. They asked what he wanted. And he answered, "I want your second sister to wife."

"How far off is your dwelling," said they.

"For such as me, ten days, and for such as you, ten years," was the answer.

"Ten years!" said they, "we won't let our sister go." But

their youngest brother again took his sister and gave her to the tiger, as he had done before with the lion.

The next day the eagle came and knocked at the door, and they asked him who was there, and he said, "I am the eagle, and have come to take your youngest sister to wife."

Him too they asked if his dwelling was far. And he answered, "For such as me, fifteen days, and for such as you, fifteen years."

"We won't let our sister go," said they. "One sister we have let go five years' journey away, the other, ten years', and shall we let this one go fifteen?"

Once more the youngest brother took her too by the hand, and gave her to the eagle.

When the maidens were married, the young men got married too; first the eldest, then the middle one, and lastly the youngest opened the chamber to take thence the fairy. But the fairy at once escaped and said to him, "If you want to get me, you must make an iron staff and iron shoes, and come

> "To the Illinees, the Billinees, the Alamalacusians. *
> Unto the marble mountains, and unto the crystal meadows."

So he made the iron staff and the iron shoes and went to find her. And when he had gone five years' journey, he came to his sister's house, and sat outside on the stone seat to rest. Then the servant came out to fill her pail with water, and he asked her for a drink from the pail. At first she would not give him one, but after he had entreated her, she did so. And while he drank the water, he dropped his ring into it. The maid brought the water to her mistress. The mistress perceived by the ring that her brother was outside.

"Whom have you given water to?" she asked her maid.

"I have not given to anyone," said the maid.

"Don't be afraid," said her mistress, "tell me who the man was?"

"He is a traveller, he was sitting on the stone seat outside," said the maid, "and he besought me, and I gave him some."

"Go and bid him come in," said she.

---

* These names are mere gibberish.

And when he was come in, they embraced one another, and his sister asked him :

" How did you come hither ? "

Then he told her all that had befallen him. As they were talking, they heard the lion coming. " Let me hide you," said she to her brother, " lest he eat you." And she gave him a pat and he was turned into a broom, and she put him against the door.

When the lion had come in at the door, he said, " I smell kingly blood ! " .

" Kingly the ways that you walk ! " replied the King's daughter, " hence the smell of kingly blood in your nose ! " While they were eating bread, the king's daughter said to the lion, " If my eldest brother were to come, what would you do to him ? "

" I would rip him up," said he.

" If the second one were to come ? "

" I would make mince-meat of him."

" If the youngest came ? "

" I would kiss him on his eyes."

" He has come ! " said she.

" And you hide him from me ? " said he. Then she took the broom and gave it a pat, and it became her brother.

The lion embraced him, kissed him, and asked him wherefore he was come.

Then he told him all that had befallen him, and asked him if he knew where were the

" Illinees, the Billinees, the Alamalacusians,
The mountains made of marble, and the meadows all of crystal."

" I don't know them myself," said he, " but to-morrow I will summon all the beasts, and perhaps one of them may know."

On the morrow he summoned all the beasts, but none of them knew. So he set off the next day to find the "Illinees, Billinees," and after five years he came to the other sister, and sat again on the stone seat, and the maid-servant came to fetch water, and he begged her to give him a little water from the pail to drink.

And when he had drunk, he dropped his ring into the pail, and when his sister saw the ring, she perceived that it belonged to her brother, and she sent, and they called him in. And when he was come in they embraced and kissed each other, and his sister asked him, "How did you come?" And when he had told her all that had befallen him, they heard the tiger coming. And she gave him a pat, and turned him into a dust-box, so that the tiger might not eat him. As soon as the tiger came in, "I smell kingly blood!" says he.

"Kingly the ways that you walk," said his wife to him. "hence the smell of king's blood in your nostrils. If my eldest brother were to come, what would you do to him?"

"I would rip him up," said he.

"If the second one came?"

"I would make mince-meat of him," said he.

"And if the youngest came?"

"I would treat him as a brother."

"He has come," said she, "and I was afraid you would eat him, and so I hid him." Then she gave him another pat, and made him into a man. Thereupon the tiger embraced him, and kissed him, and asked him, "Wherefore are you come?"

He asked him whether he knew of the "Illinees, Billinees."

"I don't know them," said he. "To-morrow, I will summon all the beasts, and some of them may know."

So in the morning he summoned them, but none of them knew.

So next day he set off, and came to his third sister, who was five years' journey further still. And again he went and sat on the stone seat by his sister's house ; and the maid came to fetch water, and he begged a drink, and threw his ring into the pail. And when the King's daughter saw the ring, she perceived that her brother had come, and sent her maid to bid him come in. And when he was come in, they embraced and kissed each other, and she asked him, "Wherefore are you come?" And he told her what had befallen him. Then came the eagle, and asked why he was come.

And he told him, and asked him if he knew of the "Illinees, Billinees."

"I know them not," said he ; "but to-morrow I will gather together all the birds, and perhaps one of them may know."

So on the morrow all the birds were gathered together, and the eagle asked them if they knew anything about the " Illinees, Billinees." "We know them not," said they; "but there is a lame she-hawk absent, and perhaps she may know."

Then the lame she-hawk came, and she did know. Then said the eagle to her, "Take this man to the 'Illinees, Billinees.'" "I will," said the lame she-hawk. And when they came to the " Illinees, Billinees," the iron shoes were worn to holes. So he came to the " Illinees, Billinees," and found his bride, who was with other fairies, and he took her to his palace, and married her.

THE LITTLE BROTHER WHO SAVED HIS SISTER FROM THE DRAGON.

(EPIRUS.)

——— :0: ———

ONCE upon a time there was a King who had three sons and one daughter. At the foot of his palace there was a garden, and into the garden a dragon used to come.

The Princess did not like to go into the garden, because she feared the dragon might take her. One day, her youngest brother took her, and they went into the garden. Suddenly the dragon appeared, and bore her aloft into the air, and took her up into a high mountain, whither no one could ascend. When he had taken the Princess, the King put the whole palace in mourning, and held no courts of justice; only the ministers held the courts.

The youngest brother, since it was his fault that the dragon had taken his sister, resolved to go and find her, or to perish. His father would not let him go, for he loved him more than all the others. But he could not rest, and was determined to go and find her. At length, after some days, he set off, and came to the foot of the mountain, but he could not get up to the top.

There, at the foot of the mountain, he found two snakes fighting, one black, and the other white. And the black one was on the point of killing the white one, which when he perceived, he slew the black one; and then the white one said to him,

"What good thing can I do for you, for the kindness you have shown to me?"

"I want nothing else," said the Prince, "but that you should put me up on the top of this mountain."

"Fasten yourself to my tail," said the snake. So when he had fastened himself to its tail, it took him to the top of the mountain, and then disappeared. The Prince went to a shepherd who was feeding the dragon's sheep, and entered the service of the shepherd, and put on herdsman's clothes. The shepherd used to send him every week to the dragon to fetch bread.

One day he found his sister alone, and said to her, "I am your brother, and am come to fetch you."

"And how did you get here?" she said, "were you not afraid lest the dragon should eat you? He may come any moment, so you had better hide, lest he find you. To flee hence is impossible, and we cannot escape from the clutches of the dragon; for his chambers are filled with princesses whom he has enthralled and we cannot get down from the mountain. Nay, I wonder how you could have got up, for not even a bird can do so."

"I fastened myself to a snake's tail," said he, "and so I got up. This evening, when the dragon comes, ask him where his strength lies, and, whatever he tells you, let me know to-morrow when I come."

In the evening, the dragon came, and the Princess asked him where his strength lay. And the dragon told her that he had three golden hairs in his head, and with these a chamber might be opened, and in the chamber were three doves: if one died, the dragon would fall sick; if the other, he would get very ill; and if the third, he would die.

Next day, when her brother came, she told him these things, and he said to her, "In the evening, next time you are combing out his hair, take a pair of scissors and cut off the golden hairs, and open the chamber and kill the doves, so that the dragon may die." At eventide the Princess waited till the dragon was asleep, and cut off the hairs, and opened the chamber, and killed the doves, and the dragon died.

When the dragon was dead, they opened all the rooms, and set free all the people whom he had enthralled. They set free, among the rest, three princesses, and these they took with them. And when they had got to the brow of the mountain, they saw their brothers, who were waiting at the foot; and he hung down the hairs, and first let down the eldest princess, and cried, "This is the bride of our eldest brother!" Then he let down the second, and cried, "This is the second one's bride!" Last of all he let down the youngest, and said that was his own.

When his brothers saw that the youngest was fairer than the rest, they envied him, and cut the hairs, and left him on the top of the mountain.

In his grief he returned to the palace of the dragon, and walked through the chambers. In one chamber, which was carpeted green, he saw a velvet greyhound hunting a velvet hare. In another chamber he saw a golden basin, and a golden jug which poured water of itself. In another chamber he saw a golden nest, with golden birds. Afterwards, he went into the stables, and in one stable he saw three horses with golden wings, one grey, another red, and another green.

"What kindness shall we show you," said the horses, "for opening the door for us?"

"I want nothing more," said he, "than that you should get me away from the mountain."

"Get on my back," said the green one; and when he had mounted him, he scoured across the hill and put him down in the plain. Then each of the three horses gave him a golden hair, and said to him, "When you want us, set fire to a hair, and we will come."

After walking for some days, he came to the state where his father was King.

And he put a bladder on his head, so that they took him. for a scab-pate, and he hired himself to a goldsmith.

When they had brought the Princess and her two brothers to their father, along with the other three princesses, he asked them, "What has become of your youngest brother?" and they told him he was dead.

The eldest prince tried to force the eldest princess to marry him; but she refused, and said she would not marry unless he made the velvet greyhound hunt the velvet hare, which was in the dragon's dwelling. And the King issued a proclamation, asking who was able to do this. Then the scab-pate said to the goldsmith that he would do it, and begged he might go to offer his services to the King. After offering to do what was desired, the scab-pate asked them to provide him with a measure of good wine and a measure of chestnuts (roasted), and to let him shut himself up alone in his room. So they brought him everything he asked, and he shut himself up in his room. The goldsmith watched at the key-hole to see how he would manage matters. The scab-pate did nothing but eat chestnuts and drink wine. Then the goldsmith went away and fell asleep. At day-break the scab-pate lit a hair (of the grey horse), and the horse came.

"What do you want with me?" it said.

"I want you," said he, "to bring me the greyhound and the hare."

And straightway he brought it, and in the morning he gave it to the goldsmith. The goldsmith sent him with it to the King, and the King, when he got it, loaded him with money. But he gave the money to the goldsmith.

On the Sunday, when the marriage was to take place, every one went out into the country to play at javelins on horseback. When the goldsmith had left his workshop and gone out for a walk, the scab-pate lit a hair, and straightway the green horse came, and brought him a green robe. Then the scab-pate rode forth afield to play at javelins.

When he had played for some time, and was about to go away, they rushed at him to catch him; but he strewed silver and gold on the ground, and fled back to the workshop, and put his head again into the bladder.

The next Sunday the second brother wanted to be married, and to wed the second princess. But she said she would not marry unless they brought her the gold basin and the golden jug which were in the palace of the dragon. Then the King sent an order to all the goldsmiths, that whoever was able should produce them.

Again the scab-pate promised to get them, and told his master to get him two measures of chestnuts and two measures of wine; and when he had got them for him, he sat till morning eating chestnuts and drinking wine.

And at morning he lit a hair, and the red horse came, and he bade it bring him the golden basin and the golden jug. The horse brought them at once, and the scab-pate took them to the King, and the King loaded him with money. Again they went to play javelins when the second wedding took place. The scab-pate lit a hair, and the red horse came and brought him a red robe.

And when he had dressed himself, he, too, went to play javelins. After playing a long time, he started to go away, and then they rushed to catch him. Then he flung money down, and they let him go.

Next Sunday, the youngest sister was to be married, and was to wed a brother of the King; but she refused, and said unless they brought her the golden nest with the golden eggs, she would not marry. These, too, the scab-pate brought, and on the Sunday, when they were to be married, they went out to play javelins. The scab-pate went, too, with the grey horse, and with a white robe. And while they were playing, he threw his javelin and killed his uncle. Then they took him and brought him to the King. And the King asked him why he had slain his uncle. Then he told him all that he had suffered. And when the King heard it, he forthwith gave orders to slay his two other sons; and to the youngest he gave the youngest princess, and they lived happily ever afterwards.

THE BET WITH THE BEARDLESS.

(EPIRUS.)

—— :0: ——

THERE was once a father who had three sons, of whom the youngest was lame.

And when the father died, he left them as legacy a warning never to travel with any one beardless or lame. "Good, Sire," said his sons.

When the father was dead, the eldest sets out on a journey. When he had gone some little way from home he found a Beardless One, who asked him, "Whither away, my son?"

"I am going a journey," he answered.

"Won't you take me with you?" says the Beardless One.

"No, I will not," says he, "for our father left word with us that we were never to travel with anyone who was beardless."

He goes on and finds another Beardless One, and tells him the same. He goes further and meets yet another. The Beardless One asks him, "Whither away, my son?"

"On a journey."

"Won't you take me with you?"

Then he thinks to himself, "I meet nothing but beardless men, and I may meet more still. Suppose I take him." So he says to the Beardless One, "Come along, then."

On the way they agree that whichever of them gets angry, the other shall cut the flesh from his back.

After a time the Beardless One gives him a roll of bread, and says to him, "You see this roll? Eat it and give it to the dog, and keep it whole." Then says the other, "How, then, should the roll remain whole?"

"There you are," says the Beardless One, "you see, you've lost your temper!"

And he stopped and cut the flesh from his back, and so the poor fellow went away.

The same thing befell the second son also.

Then the youngest, the lame one, started. After starting he found three Beardless Ones like his brothers, and with the third he made the same bargain. Then the Beardless One gave him the roll of bread, and said to him, "There's some bread. Eat it yourself and give it to my dog, and yet keep it whole."

Then what does the cunning fellow do?

He goes down to the herd of the Beardless One (for he was tending it at the time), kills a lamb, roasts it and eats it.

The dog began to bark, so he takes it and kills it. After that he passed a wain with some bullocks; and one of the bullocks was near dying; so he changed the two that were yoked to the wain for two of his own, and asked the men who had the wain, " Have you got any bread and wine ? "

" We have," said they. Then he slew a heifer, and roasted it, and they ate and drank. And when he took the herd home to the Beardless One, the latter, on seeing that some were missing, made no complaint, but only said, "Now I have found my match."

But when the Lame One had treated the Beardless One in this manner several times, he could bear it no longer, and said to the former, " What has become of the cattle ? "

The Lame One said, " According to our bargain, you must not complain. Now stand still while I cut a slice of flesh from your back." So he cut the flesh from his back, took away the Beard-less One's goods, and went home.

——————— ——

THE KNIFE OF SLAUGHTER, THE WHET-
STONE OF PATIENCE, AND THE
UNMELTING CANDLE.

(Epirus.)

————:o:————

There was once a rich man who had an only daughter, who sat embroidering at the window. And while she was embroidering, a bird passed, and said to her :

" Why embroiderest thou and gildest ? Thou shalt wed a lifeless husband."

Then the girl goes weeping to her father, and tells him all the bird had said to her.

And her father answered, " 'Tis but a bird ; let it warble as it will."

But the bird came many times to the window, and always said the same ; and the girl went to her father and told him all that it said, as at first.

And one day, when she was with her companions playing out of doors, a shower of rain caught them, and they stood under the eaves of a neighbouring house, and while they stood there the door opened and she went in, and again the door shut of itself. And while she dwelt there by herself, she passed by the rooms in turn, and there, in one room, she found a dead Prince, and he had a letter in his hand, whereon something was written, which she read and which ran as follows :

" Whosoever shall come hither and watch for three weeks, and three days, and three hours without sleeping, I will arise, and if it is a man I will make him my vizier, and if it is a woman I will take her to wife."

Then she, when she had so read, sat three weeks and three

days without sleeping, and afterwards she saw a gipsy woman below, and she bade her come up to the window, and said to her, "Sit here for two hours while I sleep, and when the two hours are over, wake me up."

"Good," said the gipsy woman.

So she fell asleep, but the gipsy did not wake her, but sat up the three hours herself. And afterwards the Prince awoke and said to the gipsy, "You are my wife."

Then the gipsy said to him, "Take her who is asleep, and set her to feed the geese." So he took her and set her to feed the geese.

One day an order came for him to go to the wars, and he called his wife and asked her what she wished him to bring her.

And she told him he was to bring her a golden dress.

Then he called her who fed the geese, and asked her, "Do you wish me to bring you anything on my return?"

And she said to him, "I want you to bring me the Knife of Slaughter, the Whetstone of Patience, and the Unmelting Candle, else may your horse refuse to stir."

Then he set off and went to the wars, and conquered the foe.

And when he turned back he took the golden garment for his wife, but forgot to take for her who fed the geese what she had told him.

And when he was about to start, his horse refused to stir. Then he sat down and pondered. At last he remembered the things that she who fed the geese had bid him bring, and he went to the bazaar asking for them, and found them in a shop and bought them.

And the merchant who sold them, said to him, "For whom are you getting them?" "For my maid," said the Prince. "When you give them her, see what she will do," said he.

And the Prince took them and came to his country, and on his arrival his wife asked him, "Have you brought me what I told you?"

"I have," said the Prince, and gave her the golden garment.

He also gave the girl who fed his geese, the knife, the whetstone, and the candle. And she took them and went to her hut and shut herself in, and put the Whetstone of Patience on the ground, and upon it she placed the Knife of Slaughter, and lit the Unmelting Candle, and set it near the knife.

And the Prince drew near, and watched to see what she would do. And she began to say :

" Why dost thou tarry, oh Knife of Slaughter ? Wilt thou not arise and cut my throat ? "

Then the knife rose to cut her throat, but the Whetstone of Patience turned it back, and when the knife began to rise, the Unmelting Candle began to go out.

" I was a Grandee's daughter," she continued, " and while I was embroidering, there would come a bird, and would say to me : ' Why embroiderest thou and gildest ? Thou shalt have a lifeless husband,' and I believed it not. Why dost thou tarry, oh knife ? Wilt thou not rise and cut my throat ? "

(Then the knife rose and the whetstone turned it back.)

" And once as I was playing with my companions, a shower caught us and I stood at the door of this palace, until the rain should be over. Why dost thou tarry, Knife of Slaughter, and arisest not to cut my throat ? "

(Then the knife rose up above her, but the whetstone turned it back.)

" And the door opened and took me in, and I walked through all the rooms until I came to the Prince's room, and saw the letter which he held in his hand and read it. Why tarryest thou, Knife of Slaughter, and risest not and cuttest off my head ? "

(And it rose above her, but the Whetstone of Patience turned it back.)

" And I sat for three weeks and three days without sleeping : and then the gipsy, whom he has for his wife, came by the window, and I bade her come up, and told her to sit and watch two hours, but she sat and watched three, and waked me not, and so the Prince took her to wife, and me he set to feed his geese. How can'st thou bear it, Knife of Slaughter, that I should sit sleepless for three weeks, and now be a feeder of geese, and the gipsy but three hours and be Princess ? Art thou yet still, oh Knife ? "

Then the Knife of Slaughter rose very high above her, so that the Whetstone of Patience could no longer reach it, and the candle all but went out.

Then the Prince when he heard it wept, and broke open the door, and seized the knife which was coming down upon the noble's daughter, and he took her and made her his wife, and set the gipsy to feed the geese.

THE FOX ON PILGRIMAGE.

(Epirus.)

:0:

There was once a Fox who had nothing to eat, so she pretended to go on a pilgrimage. On her way she met a cock, and the latter asked her,

"Where are you going, my lady?"*

"On pilgrimage and back," said she.

"Shall I come too?" said he.

"Come along," said she. "Shall I take you on my back?"

So the cock went with her.

She went on and met some doves, and when the doves saw her they fluttered with their wings. But she said to them, "Don't fly away, don't fly away, I have done with all that sort of thing. Now I am off on a pilgrimage."

"Shall I come too, my lady?" said the eldest.

"Well, as the cock is going, you may as well come too," said she. "Shall I take you on my back?" Then the doves went with her.

She went further, and met some crested larks. When the latter saw her they fluttered with their wings. "Don't fly away," said the Fox. "I have given up those old ways of mine. I am off on a pilgrimage now."

"Shall I come too?" said the eldest.

"As the others are going, you may as well come with us. Shall I take you on my back?"

When they had gone a long way they came to a cave, and there the Fox said to them, "Let us turn in here and shrive one another, for we have seas and rivers to cross, and God only

---

* In the Greek, "Lady Mary," the soubriquet answering to Reynard, Reineke, &c., among the nations of Western Europe.

knows whether we shall live to accomplish our pilgrimage or not. Come now, cock, let me shrive you."

"What have I done, my lady?" said the cock.

"What have you done!" said she. "You who crow at midnight and wake man and wife! And sometimes you crow too early and the caravans are deceived and start on their journey, and the robbers come upon them." So Mistress Fox set to work and ate the cock.

"Come, dove, let me shrive *you!*"

"What harm have I done, my lady," said the dove.

"What harm have you done!" said she. "When people sow their grain in hopes of a crop, and you go and scrape it up and eat it?" So she ate the dove.

Lastly she called the crested lark.

"Come, crested lark, let me shrive you."

"What harm have I done, my lady?" said he.

"What harm have you done!" said she. "You who have stolen the king's crown, and wear it on your head?"

"Nay, my lady," said he, "wait till I go and bring witnesses."

"Very well, off with you."

So the crested lark goes and sits on a wild pear tree, and there came by a hunter who aimed at him with his gun, and thought to kill him.

"Don't kill me," says he, "and you will have your reward. Come, I will show you where a Fox is hiding."

So he took him and brought him to the place, and as he came to the mouth of the cave the crested lark called out, "Come forth, my lady, I have brought you witnesses."

Then said the Fox, "So, so! But won't these witnesses deign to come in?"

"No, they don't wish to enter. Will your ladyship kindly come out?"

And the hunter pointed his gun at the mouth of the cave, and when the Fox prepared to come out the huntsman fired at her, and killed her, and as she lay in her last struggle the Fox said to the crested lark, "Woe worth the day and the witnesses that you brought me."

THE HUSBANDMAN, THE SNAKE, AND THE FOX.

(EPIRUS.)

—— :o: ——

THERE was a husbandman working on his field, and in the middle of the field there was a heap of stones. And he said to himself, "I will cut up the brambles, and clear away the stones, and make that spot also into a tilled field." Just as he was about to set fire to the brambles, there appeared a snake in the midst of them, who said to him, "Beware that you burn not my house."

"Nonsense, I shall burn it," said the husbandman.

"Be it so, then," said the snake. "Burn my house if you like, only put your staff down in the bramble bush so that I may have a path to walk out by."

And while the husbandman was holding the staff the snake passed up it and coiled itself round him. Then the husbandman proposed to the snake that they should go and have the matter tried before three judges. First they found a horse and said to him, "Such and such is the case between us."

Then the horse said, "When I was with my master and enjoyed my youth, they used to ride me and kept me in the stall. Now they have turned me adrift into the wilderness : and now the time has come for the snake to eat you." They went further and they found a mule, and he told them the same. Lastly, they find a fox, and say to her, "Come, my lady, let us be tried by you, for we have a difference."

"How can I judge between you while one is riding the other. Come down upon the ground apart, and then I will judge you."

So the snake came down on to the ground.

Then says my lady to the husbandman, "What are you waiting for now, my friend : take a pitchfork and give him a prog or two on the head, and send him about his business, and I will help you." The husbandman takes his staff, gives the snake a blow and kills it. Then says the husbandman to the fox, " How shall I show my thanks for the kindness you have done me ? "

" I want nothing else," said she, " but a few young chickens, if you have them."

" Good ! I will bring them you," said he. So he goes home, finds his wife, and says to her :

" My love, I was in such and such a plight, and my lady fox got me out of the scrape ; and now I want to bring her a brood of young chickens." Then said his wife to him :

" What a fool you are, husband ! Why don't you take your hounds, and put them in the bag, and go and catch her." So the man took the hounds and put them in the bag and went.

My lady was waiting. Just as she turned out the bag to seize the chickens, out tumbled the hounds and caught her and tore her sadly. And she, as she slunk into her hole, exclaimed, " Neither my grandfather nor my father was ever a magistrate, but I must turn magistrate and judge men's quarrels for them !" Be wiser, my lady. another time !

THE PRINCESS WHO WENT TO THE WARS.

(EPIRUS.)

————:o:————

THERE was once a King who had three daughters. Once there came a message for him to go to war. As he was an old man, he sat down and wept, and pondered what he should do. Then his eldest daughter came to him and said, "What ails you, father, that you weep?".

"It's nothing that concerns you to know: only get you hence," said he.

"Nay, sire, but tell me. I will know."

"What shall I tell you, poor girl?" said he. "See! they have sent word for me to go to the war, and I am too weak."

"Oh! out upon the war and worse luck to it," said his daughter. "Why I was expecting you to get me married!"

Then the middle daughter comes and asks him, "What ails you, father, that you weep?"

"Get you hence!" says he. "It concerns you not to know."

"Nay, but tell me, what it is."

"I won't tell you, for you will say to me as your sister did."

"Nay, sire, I will not say what my sister said."

"Well!" says he, "this is what ails me, my darling. They have sent word for me to go to war, and I am too old and weak to go."

"Oh! woe betide the war and worse luck to it!" said the girl. "I was expecting you to get me married!"

Then the youngest comes and asks him, "What ails you, father, that you weep?"

"Get you hence," says he. "It is no concern of yours to know."

"Nay, but tell me," said she.

"I won't," said he, "for you will talk like the rest."

"No!" said she, "whatever happens to me, I will not talk like them."

"See then what ails me, girl" said he, "they have sent me word to go to the war, and I cannot go, for I am too old."

"And is that why you sit and weep, my father?" says she. "Make me a man's dress, and give me a good horse, and I will go to the war."

"Get you hence!" said the King. "A girl like you go to war!"

"Nay, never heed!" said the Princess, "I will go and conquer."

"Be it so!" said the King; so he made her a Frankish suit, and gave her a good steed, and the Princess went to the war and overcame the foe.

In that war there was with her a Prince from another kingdom : and when they came back from the war they went and stayed at that Prince's palace. Then the Prince recognised the Princess as no young man, and said to his mother, "Only think, mother, a maiden in the battle-field!"

And his mother said to him, "Why, my son, how can a girl go to war?"

But he said it was a girl.

So his mother said to him, "Go out and sleep both of you on the grass, and if your place is the greener she is a maiden ; but, if not, she is a man."

Then they went out into the meadow and lay down to sleep : and when the Prince had fallen asleep, she went to another place a long way off, and on the morrow at early dawn she came back to her first place, and when they arose they looked, and behold, the place where the Princess lay was greener. Then he went to his mother, and told her that his place was the drier of the two. Then said his mother, "Didn't I tell you it was a man?"

"Nay," said he again, "it is a maid." And when the Princess was departing to go to her own kingdom, and had got beyond the boundary, she cried, "A maiden I went to the war, a maiden I come back, to shame the son of that donkey of a king."

When the Prince heard that, he said to his mother, "Did I not say so, mother? She is a girl. I will go to her kingdom to fetch her."

Then he put on mean attire and took spindle-shafts and spindles and collars, and went and sold them in the country of the Princess, and kept calling. "Spindle-shafts and spindles and collars for 'Golden Tooth.'" For he knew that they had taken out one of the Princess' teeth and had put her in one of gold. When the handmaids of the Princess heard these words that he was calling, they said to the Princess, "Mistress, do you hear what that good-for-nothing fellow is calling?"

" Let him jabber," said the Princess.

" Shall we not take any thing?" said the maids.

" Take what you will," said the Princess.

Then they asked him his price for a collar. But he said :

" I want no money, only a pan of millet."

So they gave him a pan of millet, and just as he was going to put it in his bag, he spilt it and sat down to pick it up grain by grain, until nightfall.

Then the maids said to him, "Why don't you ask us for another pan of millet, rather than sit there picking it up?"

" Nay," said he, "this must be my first business : only put me into a garret to sleep."

And they brought him to the Princess, and she said to them " Put him into a garret and let him sleep."

Then he watched to see where they put the keys, that shut the apartment of the Princess : and he went by night and took the keys and opened the chamber-door and flung a sleeping-herb upon the Princess, which he had with him, and took her on his back, and carried her off to his own country.

And when the Princess awoke and found herself in a strange place, she did not speak for three years. Then the Prince's mother said to him :

" You must have lost your wits to go and bring us that deaf and dumb woman. Now you had better leave her and take another."

However they plighted their troth to each other, and when he was going to be married to the other, they gave a candle to the deaf and dumb girl just as they did to the rest, and when the candle burnt down she did not throw it away, but kept it in her hand.   And the rest said to her :

"Your hand's on fire, Dummy!"

And she made as though she did not hear.   Then the bridegroom said :

"Bid the bride say it to her also."

So the bride said, "Dummy, your hand is on fire."

"May you be dumb, and go back to the place whence you came," she answered.   "I spake but one word to the Prince and have been silent for three years, and you in your bridal garland dare to call me 'Dummy?'"

Then when the Prince heard these words he left the bride he was about to take, and took the "dumb girl," and so they lived happily all their lives.

THE TWINS.

(EPIRUS.)

———:o:———

THERE was once a fisherman who had no children. One day an old woman called on the fisherman's wife and said to her :

"What is the use of all your wealth to you when you have no children ? "

" God has so willed it, good dame," said the fisherman's wife.

" Nothing of the sort, my child," said the old woman, "it is your husband's fault; for if he were to catch the golden fish, he would have children. When your husband comes home at night tell him to go and catch it, if you want to have children. And you must cut it in six pieces. One piece you must eat yourself, and one your husband must eat, and you will have two children. One the bitch must eat, and she will have two puppies. One the mare must eat, and she will have two foals. One you must put on the curb-stone at one corner of your house, and one at the other, and two cypress-trees will spring up."

In the evening, when her husband came, his wife told him all this, and off he went at once and caught the fish, and did with it as the old woman had directed. After some time he had two boys so like each other that they could not be distinguished. The bitch had two puppies just like each other, the mare two foals, and at the curb-stones grew two cypress trees. When the lads were grown up they would not stay at home, but wanted to go and make a name for themselves. The father would not let them go, because they were his only children, and said to them, " Let one go first alone, and when he has come back let the other go." Then one of them took one of the dogs and one of the horses and set off, and said to his brother that as long as one of the cypress trees remained green, he should consider him safe and sound ; but should it wither, he must go in search of him.

He went on and on a long way from his home, till he came and stopped at an old woman's house. At even-tide, as he sallied forth for a while, he said to the old woman, "Whose is that house over there?"

And the old woman answered, "That is the house of the Fair One of the Land."

"And I," said the youth, "have come to fetch her."

"Many, my son," said she, "have come to fetch her, but none have succeeded, and she has cut off their heads and impaled them on those iron spikes that you see sticking upright there."

Then said the youth to her, "I will go and tell her I will fetch her, though she cut off my head."

Now the lad knew well how to play the guitar. So he played it that evening and the Princess heard it.

In the morning the Fair One of the Land said to the old woman, "Good dame, whom have you staying with you, who was playing the guitar so beautifully?"

"A stranger has come, my lady," said the old woman, "and it was he who was playing it."

"Tell him to come and let me see him," said the Princess.

So the youth went to the Princess, and she asked him whence he was, and told him how much the guitar pleased her, and that she was willing to marry him.

"And I, Princess," says the youth, "have come for this very purpose."

"Go and tell my father," said she, "that you wish to take me to wife, and what he tells you, come and tell to me."

So the youth went to the King, and told him he wished to take the maiden to wife.

And the King said to him, "If you are able to do whatsoever I tell you, well; but if not, I shall take your head. I have a thick block of wood in the field, which two hairs' length will not compass. Hew it in twain with one stroke of your sword, and I will give you my daughter in marriage; but otherwise I shall take your head."

So the lad arose and went sorrowfully away to the old woman because next day the King was going to cut off his head. That evening he did not play the guitar, which he was wont to play every evening, but kept thinking how he should hew so big a block in twain.

When the Princess heard no guitar, she called to him : " Why do you not play the guitar, but are so sad ? "

Then the youth told her all the King had said to him.

" And is .that why you are grieved ? " said the Princess. " Quick, play your guitar, that we may enjoy ourselves a little, and to-morrow morning come and call on me."

So the youth played the guitar all the evening, and they had a right joyous time of it ; and on the morrow, at daybreak, the Princess gave him a hair from her tresses, and told him to twine it round his sword, and he would hew the block. So the lad went to the place where the block lay, and, at one stroke, he hewed it in twain. And the King said to him, " Yet one thing more I must tell you to do, and I will give you my daughter to wife. You must ride a horse, and go for three hours at a gallop, and you must hold in your hands two pails full of water, and if you don't spill a single drop, I will give you my daughter to wife, but otherwise I shall take your head." Again the youth went away sorrowful to the old woman, and did not play the guitar. Then the Princess called to him, and said to him, " Why do not you play the guitar, this evening, but are so sad ? "

Then he told her what the King had said to him. And the Princess told him not to be sad, but to play the guitar as usual, and on the morrow to come to her.

On the morrow he went, and the Princess gave him her ring. and said to him, " You must put this ring into the water, and it will freeze, and so will not be spilt." Then he did as the Princess had told him, and the water was not spilt.

And when he saw it was not spilt, the King said to him, " Yet one thing more I have to tell you, and after that I shall say no more. I have a negro, and to-morrow you must wrestle together, and if you overcome him, you shall take the Princess."

Then the youth went merrily to the Princess, and was full of joy. The Princess calls to him, and says, " You seem pretty merry this evening. What has my father said to you, to make you so merry?" And the lad said, "He told me I am to wrestle with a negro, and I hope to overcome him, for he is a man and so am I."

" That is the worst of all," said the Princess, " for I am the negro. They give me a sherbet to drink, and I become a negro. However, go to-morrow to the market, and buy twelve thongs of ox-hide to harness your horse, and take this handkerchief too. When I come against you, show it me, that I may have an inkling who you are, and not kill you. Try to strike my steed between the eyebrows, and when you have slain my steed, you will have conquered me."

So he went to wrestle with the negro.

And when they had wrestled and eleven of the thongs of ox-hide had snapped, and the negro was making ready to slay the lad, the latter smote the negro's steed between the eyebrows, and when his steed had fallen dead upon the arena, the negro was overcome, and the youth had conquered. And the King said to him :

" Now that you have done this, I will make you my son-in-law."

The lad said to him, " I have some business at present, but after a hundred days, I will come and fetch her."

So the youth went elsewhere, and came to a town, and stopped at an old woman's house.

And in the evening they supped, and the lad asked the old woman for water. " I have none," said she, " we only get water here once a year, for a monster has it in keeping, and every year we give him a maiden to eat, and he lets us fetch water. And now the lot has fallen on the King's daughter, and they will bring her to the monster, to-morrow."

Next day they brought the King's daughter for the monster to eat, and they tied her up near his dwelling with a golden chain, and went away and left her there alone.

When they had all gone away, the youth went to the Princess, and found her weeping, and asked her, " What ails you that you weep ? " And the Princess said to him, that the monster would come forth and eat her, and that was why she wept.

And the youth said to her that he would rescue her if she would take him for her husband.

Then the Princess said she would.

And when the monster came forth, the youth gave the word to his dog, and he throttled the monster, and so the Princess was saved.

And when the King learnt that, he himself also resolved to give his daughter to wife to the youth, and they celebrated the wedding. When the youth had been a week in the house, he got weary and wanted to go forth to hunt. The King did not want him to go, but he could bear the confinement no longer. He told him to take attendants with him, but he would not, and took only his horse and his dog.

And when they had gone some way, and he felt thirsty, and espied a hut at some distance, he went thither to drink water.

And in the hut was an old woman, and he asked her to give him a little water to drink.

And the old woman bade him first let her crack a whip over his dog, and then she would give him water. So he said, "Crack away!"

And she cracked the whip over the dog, and turned him into marble; and then she turned him into marble, and turned his horse into marble, too.

And when she had turned him into marble, the cypress by the house withered.

And his other brother set off to find him, and passed by the town where his brother had slain the monster, and chanced to come and stay with the old woman with whom his brother had stayed. And when the old woman saw him she said, "Pray forgive me, my son, that I did not come to wish you joy at your wedding, when you married the King's daughter." For the old woman thought he was his other brother. "Never mind! It is no matter," said he. And he went straight away to the King's residence. And when the King saw him, he said, "What has become of you? we thought some evil had befallen you, that you have not been seen all these days."

In the evening, when he slept with the Princess, he put his sword betwixt them. And the Princess said to him, "What ails you, that you are vexed?" But he answered her not a word;

and on the morrow he went again to the hunt, and chanced to take the very way which his brother had taken, and from afar he espied his brother turned to marble, and he knew him. He went to the hut, and told the old woman to unmarble his brother.

The old woman said to him, "Let me have a crack at your dog with my whip, then I will unmarble your brother." The lad said to his dog, "Gulp down the old woman whole."

And the old woman said to him, "Tell your dog not to eat me, and I will unmarble your brother."

"Tell me how to unmarble him," said the youth, "or I will make my dog swallow you."

And as she would not, he gave the word to his dog, and he gulped her down half way. Then said the old woman to him, "I have two whips: one green, the other red. With the green one I turn to marble, and with the red one I unmarble." Then he took the red whip and unmarbled his brother, the dog, and the horse. Then he gave the word to his dog, and he finished gulping down the old woman. Then they set off, and made for the house of the father-in-law.

On the way, as they were walking, his brother told him what had befallen him, and how he had slept with his wife, but he never got so far as to tell him how he had put the sword betwixt them, for he fetched him a blow at once, and slew him, and went to his father-in-law's alone.

In the evening, when he lay down beside the Princess, she said to him, "What ailed you last night, that you would not speak to me, and put a sword betwixt us, and would not turn my way at all?"

"It was not I last night, at all," said he, "but my brother, and when he told me, on the way, that he had slept with you, I slew him." "What?" said she, "you slew him; and do you know where he is, or not?"

"I know," said he.

"To-morrow, let us go and see him," said the Princess.

So in the morning they went, and took with them a flask of "deathless water," and sprinkled it on him, and he arose again.

And when he had arisen, the other said to him :

" Forgive me, brother, for slaying you."

Then they embraced, and went to the Fair One of the Land, and he gave her to his brother in marriage, and sent word also to their parents, and they came thither also.

THE GOAT-GIRL.

(EPIRUS.)

——— :0:————

THERE was once a husbandman with his wife who had no children. His wife besought God to give her a child, though it were no better than a kid. In course of time she accordingly gave birth to a kid. It grew up and became a fine she-goat. Her mother said to her, once on a time, "Who will take water for your father to the field?" Said she, "Fasten it to my horn, and I will take it." So she fastened it, and she took it to her father. On her return, she found a sunny spot, where she took off her hide to clean it.

As a Prince passed by to go to the chase, he saw her, and his eyes were dazzled with her beauty, which shone like the sun. When she saw the Prince, she straightway went into her hide, and set off home. The Prince sent people to follow her, and watch where she went in. Then the Prince returned to his mother, and said, "Send to say I am suitor for the hand of the she-goat."

When his mother heard that she began to wail, and beat her breast, and said, "My son, if you want to marry, take a princess."

"Nay," said he, "but I will take her."

His mother saw his distress and affliction, and sent two women to get the goat. The mother of the she-goat took a cudgel to them. "Why have you come to mock me?" said she, "me, who have no daughter, only this goat that God has given me to console me!"

So the women went back and told the treatment they had met with.

The Prince said to his mother, "Go yourself."

So, willy-nilly, she went, and said to the she-goat's mother, "There's no help for it!"

The latter was so frightened when she saw the Queen, that she let her have the goat. So the Queen took her and brought her to her son. Then her son was glad, for he had eaten no bread for five days for grief.

One day the Queen made ready to knead a cake : the she-goat came with her horn and tore the dough to bits : so the Queen hit her a whack with the rolling-pin.

The next day the maid took the bread and put it into the oven. The she-goat went frisking by her side, and when she reached the oven, the goat went and spoiled the loaf with her horn. The cook seized the shovel and hit her a bang with it.

At that time a cousin of the King was to be married, and her father invited his kinsfolk to the wedding. So they made ready and went to the wedding, and tied the goat to a bench. When they were all gone, and the goat was left by herself, she, too. laid aside her hide, and dressed herself in golden embroidery, and went to the wedding, and sat by her mother-in-law. When her mother-in-law saw her beauty, she said to herself, " Would that such an one were my son's wife !" So she asked her, " Whence do you come, my child ? "

" From the rolling-pin !" said she.

She went down to the dance, and danced. When her betrothed saw her he knew her, and when the dance slackened, she flung down a golden apple, and put on her hide, and fled. In the evening, the Queen came home with her son, and said, " Did you see a fair woman at the dance ? "

Said her son, " I did ; but did not you ask her whence she came ?"

And she said, " Yes : but I don't know what she said ; I did not hear aright."

" If she come to-morrow, mind you ask her, mother !" said her son.

On the morrow, they all went again to the marriage festivities, and the goat also went, and sat by her future mother-in-law.

So she asked her, " Whence come you, my child ? "

Said she, " From the fire-shovel."

Then she went down to the dance, and danced. When the dance slackened, again she flung down a golden apple, so as to astonish the people, that she might get away. Again she put on her hide, and sat down, tied by the bench. The Prince did not know how to get the hide off her.

In the evening, he came home again with his mother, and asked her, " Mother, did you ask where that fair one came from ? "

" She told me, my son, but I have forgotten," said his mother.

In the morning, the Prince arose and went to the cook, and said to him, " Make the oven very hot, and don't bake bread for any one, because you give me no cake." Then he said to his mother, " Go you to the marriage feast,—I will come later on."

So they all went out, and he shut himself up in a neighbouring house. The goat puts off her hide, and goes to the feast. The Prince seizes the skin and flings it in the oven. The smell of the singeing hide came to her nostrils, and she left the dance and rushed to cast herself into the oven. The Prince burst forth and seized her—and said to her, "I don't mean you for the oven, my lady ! " And he took her in his arms and shut her in the glass-chamber. And he went no more to the feast, but stayed with her. His mother sent the nurse to see why her son did not come, and the nurse said to him, " Why did not you come to the feast ? "

He said, " I have a head-ache. Let my mother enjoy herself, and I will come in later on."

So his mother waited, but he did not come. So she set off and went home alone.

Then the Prince said to her, " See, mother ; take the key and bring me a mug from the glass-chamber."

As his mother went to open the door, the chamber shone. Then his mother uttered a loud cry, and told him there was a fairy in the chamber. And the Prince laughed, and said, " You have good eyes, mother ! "

Then he took his mother by the hand, and they went in together. And the bride came and kissed her hand. And the Prince said to her, " See, mother, that's the goat ! "

Then the Queen embraced her, and said to her, " My child, why have you not shown yourself all this long time ? "

And straightway, on the morrow, the Queen went and called all her royal kinsfolk to the wedding ; and she went and called the mother and father of the bride as well. But they were afraid lest they should behead them ; and they told the King they were afraid, and would not come. Then the King had clothes made for the mother and father, and went himself and brought them ; and the daughter came to meet them, and kissed her hand to them from the foot of the staircase, and welcomed her mother and father, and they celebrated the wedding, and lived happily.

THE BAY-BERRY.

(EPIRUS.)

————:o:————

THERE was once a man and his wife who had no children. So
the woman besought God to give her a child, though it were but
a bay-berry. Then God heard her prayer, and she gave birth to
the bay-berry. The people did not perceive it; but as they were
washing the linen one day, out fell the bay-berry, and became a
golden bay-tree, whose branches shone like the sun.

The young princes heard about this golden bay-tree, and came
to walk about it from every kingdom in the world. One Prince
made his tent close to its roots. He left his cook there, and went
to walk about with the other young princes. And the cook, too,
would go out, when the cooking was finished, to walk about the
bay-tree. Then a maiden came out of the bay-tree, with the
words :

> "Bay-tree high, and bay-tree low,
> Open to me, and out I go !"

Then she would eat of all the dishes, and afterwards took a
handful of salt and sprinkled it on the eatables, and made them
salt. Again she said :

> " Bay-tree high, and bay-tree low,
> Open to me, and in I go !"

At noon the Prince came and found the food so salt, that
there was no eating it ; so he seized the cook to cut off his head.
But the cook screamed, and cried, " Troth, master, it is none of
my doing !" Then the other princes came and besought the
Prince not to slay him, but to have pity on him ; so he let
him go.

The next day the cook made the dinner without any salt at all.
But the Bay-tree Maiden played the same trick. The Prince
came to eat, but he found it salter and worse than ever ! Then

the Prince perceived that it was not the cook's doing, but that of some one else. So he found no fault with him, but only said to him, "To-morrow, when you have cooked the dinner, get you hence, and I will stay and see who does the mischief." And he hid himself behind the bay-tree. Then he heard a voice from the bay-tree, saying:

> " Bay-tree high, and bay-tree low,
> Open to me, and out I go."

And she came out of the bay-tree and began to eat of the dishes. And when she took the salt, the Prince rushed out and seized her, saying, "So it is you, who play me this prank !"

Then he took her and brought her into his tent, and embraced her and kissed her ; and left her and went forth to walk. But she went weeping to the bay-tree and said:

> " Bay-tree high, bay-tree low,
> Open to me, and in I go !"

But the bay-tree said:

> " Hugged and kissed, no maiden may
> Enter more the golden bay ! "

And when the bay-tree had uttered these words, it withered away. When the princes saw what had happened, they fled away in wonder at the withering of the bay-tree.

But the other Prince stayed with the maiden.

They cut down orange branches and locust-tree boughs, and strewed them for a couch.

The maiden went to sleep, and the Prince departed. On the morrow she awoke and found him not. So she started to go away.

On the way she met a dervish, and said to him, " Good father, if I give you these clothes of mine, will you give me yours, and your horse ?"

" I will," said he, and he gave them her. And straightway she put them on and bestrode the horse, and overtook the Prince.

Said the Prince to her, " Master, on the way by which you went and came, tell me what you saw." Said he, " I saw a maiden weeping and sighing grievously, and saying, ' Orange branches, locust boughs, what have you done with my lost lover ? ' "

The Prince sighed. Then they went on again.

Again he asked the same question, and got the same answer. The Prince then took the dervish as a friend to his house, and said, " I am betrothed, and am about to celebrate my wedding, and wish to have you among my guests." So they went together and then he gave him a room to himself, and he stayed there.

The Prince began to make ready the feast.

They brought the bride, and just as they were about to crown her with the wedding wreath, the dervish went into an ante-chamber, and doffed the dervish dress, and donned the garment of gold, and shone like the sun.

And when she came into the room, the room was filled with light, and all were stricken with amazement. The Prince turned and beheld, and wondered, and said to the bride's kindred, " Take back the bride to her father's house, for I will live with my bonny bird as I was wont to do." So he married the Bay-tree maiden, and they lived a happy life.

THE PRINCE AND THE FAIRY.

(Epirus.)

————:o:————

There was once a King who had an only son. When he had grown up, his father made him a glass chamber, and put him there with a teacher to learn his lessons. And when he had learnt a great deal, one day they brought him home meat with a bit of bone in it. Then the lad wondered, for he had heard talk of bone, but had never seen a bone before. And he made a plaything of it. As ill-hap would have it he broke a pane of glass, and looked out and saw sky, hills, fields, rivers, and much else besides. Then he asked his teacher to take him out for a walk.

The teacher did not dare to do so for fear of the King, but told the lad to ask his father's leave. He did so, and his father gave him leave.

So he went out and paid visits to all the nobles. One day he went with the nobles to the chase, and they killed a great many hares. This pleased the lad much, and he took to going out every day alone, without a dog or any one to bear him company. One day he went a long way without finding anything.

But he met a Jew, and asked him, "Do you know of any game anywhere?"

"Yes," said the Jew, "on the top of yonder hill."

"How shall I get up?" said he.

"If you have money, I will get you up," said the other.

"I have," said he.

"Buy a buffalo's skin," said the Jew, "and I will put you in it, that the ravens may come and carry you up."

"And when I have got up, how am I to get down?" said he.

"Oh, there's a staircase to come down by," said the other. Then the ravens took him up on to the mountain. And there he found an immense plain, with no game nor anything else. Then he calls out, " Jew! you have cheated me ! there's nothing here. Now, how am I to get down ? "

" Throw me down two stones, and then I will fetch you down."

He threw him the stones, and the Jew took them, for they were of pure diamond, and ran away. Then the youth ran hither and thither, feeding himself on herbs and roots. As he was walking about he found a trap-door. He lifted it, and saw a staircase, and began to descend it. He kept descending for a whole day without reaching the bottom. At length he saw sky and earth. Descending by the staircase, he espies some very large palaces, and accordingly, his heart yearns to reach the place. The poor fellow hurried on in hopes of getting bread to eat. He continues his way till he comes upon an old man bound in chains, whose beard had grown down to his knees.

Says he to the grey-beard, " Give me to eat ! "

Says the grey-beard to him, " Loose me, and then I will give you something." " How shall I loose you ? " says he. " I am perished with hunger."

Says the old man to him, " Open the cupboard and take out a whip which is inside, and crack it, and whatever food you choose will make its appearance." So he cracked it, and the food appeared. He ate and regained his strength. He loosed the old man, and cleansed him, for he had been for years unwashed and without change of garments. One day the youth grew weary, and the old man said to him, " What ails thee, my son ? There are the keys, have a walk through the apartments."

But he kept back the keys belonging to one of the rooms. The young man walked through all the rooms and enjoyed himself thoroughly. When he had seen all the rooms, he saw one that was shut, and said to the old man, " You treat me as your son ; will you not open this room also for me ? "

" I open it for you ? " said he, " Why, there are fairies inside ! But I can tell you one thing you may do. In the room there is a hollow place filled with water, and when they come there they will strip. And if you are only quick enough to seize their clothes, you will escape, for all their strength is in their clothes."

The youth did as the old man bade him.

Then the eldest fairy went: she was afraid and did nothing. Then came the second; she, too, was afraid, and did nothing. At last the youngest and fairest came, and made a few movements in the water. He seizes her clothes and makes off with them. Said she, in her cunning, "Yours I am and yours I remain. Won't you give me my clothes?"

"No," said he.

"Ah, let me but get hold of the tip of my petticoat!" and she caught it and was about to pull it; but he, too, was a match for her. He gives her a slap, and flings her far away. Then he took her and brought her to the old man, and said to him, "I am going now to my father and mother. Have you a horse to give me?"

"I have," said he. "Go to the stable and call out, 'Halloa, halloa! winged steed come and take me to my father and mother!'"

Straightway the winged steed appeared, and he mounted it. He set the fairy also on the saddle. On their way they stopped at a certain place to eat bread; and there came by the brother of the fairy disguised as a dervish. "Where did you find those eatables?" he asked.

Then with divers cunning wiles the youth addressed him. "Yours we are, and yours we remain: but sit down to eat! Where does your strength reside?"

"In this crook here," said he. "If I were but to say, 'Crash crook,' it would slay you."

The other manages to get hold of the crook, and just cries, "Crash crook! on the dervish's head!" and kills him. Then they depart thence, the fairy in high dudgeon because he had slain her brother. They went on, and sat down to eat bread again, when her other brother came; and *his* strength resided in his turban, which changed him into air. The youth so contrived as to get hold also of his turban. He just cried, "Crash crook! on to the dervish's head!" and killed him too.

Then the fairy cried to herself, "I must work my own deliverance! No other help is left me."

They came to the young man's country. He says to a man

they met, "Run to bring the good news to the King, for now his son is coming!"

"Why," said the other, "the King's son is dead and turned to a skeleton long ago."

He went further, and sends another, who went and brought the good news.

Then they fired guns and generally made a royal rejoicing. They came to the palace. The King welcomed his son and his bride with music and other signs of festivity: and they held a grand carousal. The bride came before the King and danced with such grace that all were amazed.

The Prince would not give the fairy her clothes, for had she regained her power she would have slain them all.

Therefore the young man gave them to his mother, saying, " Mind you don't give them to her, or she will eat us all up."

But the fairy was cunning enough to get them away from her mother-in-law, and put them on. Then she said, " One! two! and away! I am not for your son!" and off she goes. The young man learnt it. He shouts and calls, but what is the use? She had got away.

Then he takes the winged steed, the crook, and the turban, and went to the place where he had found the fairy.

It so happened that her father was at war with another King, and said, " Whoever conquers him I will give him my daughter to wife."

Then he changed himself to air, for he had the turban of the dervish. He took also the crook, rushed to the war, and slew all the enemy. Then the King said to him, "Which of my daughters pleases you best?—take her." So he chose the youngest. And he turned himself into air, and while the fairy was eating bread he went and seized the morsels from her. Then she said to him, "Now that you have won me by force of arms and prowess, I can withstand you no longer."

So he married her, and took her away with him, and they went to the King, and spent together such a life as none had ever spent before.

THE GOLDEN STEED.

(ASTYPALÆA.)

———:o:———

ONCE upon a time there was a King and a priest who loved one another so much you would think they were brothers. They ate together, they drank together, they amused themselves together, and could not bear to be parted for a moment. They had everything that heart could desire; but, alas, their wives were childless, and they were always sad to think they had no heirs.

One day, while the two men were talking together, the King said, "Bless my soul, good father, how well were it for us if our wives had but children; the one a boy, the other a girl, so that we might always keep together."

"Well, indeed, O King," said the priest, "but this is not in our power, and we cannot fight with God, glory be to His name!"

But lo and behold, as the two were good men, and never did wrong to any, but gave alms to the poor, God loved them and listened to their words, and both their wives had children. Both the King and the priest were beside themselves with joy to see what they never expected—

> Now when age has forged her fetters.
> How the greybeard learns his letters.

But you see that no one should despair of the help of heaven. Well, what do you think? The time came for their wives to bring forth; and lo, they had two boys: not what they had looked for. However, they did not so much complain after all, lest heaven should be wroth with them, but they gave abundant glory to God and made great rejoicings and festivities. And the King told the priest not to be at all put out, for he would look on both the boys as his sons.

The boys grew up like tender plants, so that it was a joy for anyone to behold them; and when they had got a good size, the

King built, at his own expense, a large and a very beautiful castle, and in it he lodged the two lads, that they might be brought up together, and be fond of one another from earliest childhood. At once the children begun to love each other. They would get up in the morning, wash, and take their coffee, and go to school together like two little angels, full of grace and beauty, and everyone rejoiced to see them. Only from time to time their master used to scold them because they would come late to school. For children as they were, when they had finished their lessons in the evening, instead of lying down to sleep they began to play, and so the night was far spent before they went off to sleep. And in the morning they were not in a mood to go to school.

And so from time to time they would get a scolding from the master. So the son of the priest, who was the wider-awake and the more resolute of the two, proposed a plan by which both of them should not go to sleep at one and the same time, but one should sleep half the night and the other the other half. This plan pleased the King's son, and they settled that the Prince should learn his lessons in the evening, so as to sleep in the morning, for the morning sleep is the sweeter, and the Prince was somewhat delicate. Well planned and well done! Both of them slept safely and soundly, and woke up bright, and went to school.

But now see what happens! We have said already that the Prince learned his lessons at night while the priest's son slept. One evening, then, as he was sitting and reading at his little table, close upon midnight, the wall opened, and in flies a Genie, fit to frighten the life out of anyone who beheld him. He had two great lips—one of which reached to heaven and the other to the earth—a great nose, three yards long; but how could one describe all his features!

The poor Prince was seized with trembling (for he was a bit timid), and fell into a fainting fit. Our fine fiend of a friend, the Genie, had no sooner appeared, then he opened his stealthy hand, and left something on the table, and straightway vanished.

When the Prince had a little recovered, he got up and

approached the table, and there he found a paper packet. He took it up, but do you think his hands had the courage to unwrap it? However, after much ado, he did so, and what should he see? Wonder of wonders? He looked, and beheld the portrait of a maiden, who seemed to challenge the sun which should shine with the fairest sheen. Her beauty and her loveliness were such as none besides possessed. From that moment the Prince was seized with trembling, and gazed like one distraught upon the picture, which had smitten a deep wound in his heart. Far was the thought of sleep! He did nothing but fasten his eyes upon the picture. Alas, poor Prince, God help thee in the toils in which thou art entangled!

The priest's son wakes up, and asks him, "Why don't you go to sleep to-night?" He hastily thrusts the picture into his bosom, and makes believe that he had kept awake from over-study, and was now unable to sleep.

They sat for some time talking together, and afterwards the Prince gets up and goes to bed, but how could sleep ever rest upon his head?

The day dawns and the young Prince pretends to be unwell, and stays at home from school; but shuts himself up in the house, and sits without eating and drinking, gazing on the picture. One day follows another, and our good Prince goes from bad to worse. He grew weak and wan, and was almost at his wits' end. His poor father saw him with concern, for although the two lads were together and ate the same dishes, the priest's son was hale and hearty, while the Prince was wasting away where he stood like a candle in its socket, without any one knowing what ailed him. He asked him secretly, "My dear good son, what ails you, that you are always serious? Don't you get on well with the priest's son? What are you grieving for. You will be the death of me, if I see you so." But, bless me, he wouldn't speak a word, save, "Naught ails me. I am all right." But his heart told another tale. As the King could learn nothing from his son, he had recourse to the priest's son, and besought him to tell him if he knew anything about his child. But he knew nothing either. Only from that hour he was beset with an itching curiosity to sniff out the cause of the Prince's ailment, and how it was that he could neither eat nor drink nor sleep, but was always sitting shut up in the castle.

One day when he had taken him well to task, and could get nothing out of him, he went off as though to go to school : but took his seat out-side the door and watched. And he looked through the chink and saw the Prince with the picture before him, which he kept kissing, and saying, "Light of my eyes, I shall die for thy sake."

"Ah !" said the priest's son, " now I have caught you. 'The cunning bird is taken by the beak,' " he knocks at the door, goes in and says to him, " Well done you ! these many days I have been at you, and you could not make up your mind to tell me anything. What's that which you thrust into your bosom ? " Then his tongue was tied, and he could not utter a word. The other asked him where he found the thing in question. Then he began and told him everything, point by point, as we have related it : and said finally, " If I cannot get that maiden I shall die, brother ! I will take to the mountains, and run and run till my eyes are dry with weeping : and, if you will, come you along with me." He tries to quench the flame in his brother's breast, but you might as well have talked to the air.

Says the Prince to him, " If you wish to come with me, tell my father that I am out of spirits, and that I wish to go abroad that the melancholy which weighs on my heart may be dispelled."

The priest's son thought it well over and was afraid to tell it the King : but what could he do ? for he loved the Prince more than anything. At hearing that his son wished to go a journey the King was glad, and at once gave orders for a guard to assemble, to escort the Prince. But the two youths had their own plans, and taking as many provisions as they judged fit, and two good horses, they set off from the town with bands playing and colours flying, How could the unfortunate King know what they were up to ? They marched all that day, and at eventide they sat down to rest. Just as morning dawned the guard had eaten and drunk and fallen asleep. When the two youths saw that they were all asleep, they arose and gave them the slip.

Next morning the guard awoke, and looked for their leaders.

But where are they to be found? Far away and still on the march. The poor soldiers weep and wail, for they feared to meet the King, if they left the Prince and the priest's son to perish, but alas, there was no help for it: so they returned to town playing a funeral march. On hearing the news, the King was like to kill himself. The poor priest was nigh losing his wits. When was weeping, when was anguish like theirs? The King and the Priest wail and will not be comforted. They put on mourning, they plucked their beards in grief at the affliction that had befallen them : and all the country-side mourned with them : no song, no laughter anywhere, but everywhere sorrow and lamentation.

But let us leave them for the present, and follow the two young men, who scoured over field and hill at random. At last, after the lapse of a month, they espied a castle, and said it were well to repair thither for a little rest. So they came to the castle. They see that it is carpeted with strewn fir-boughs, and set with tables on which were dishes still smoking hot, but not a sign of any master or mistress of the house. They say to one another, "Let us sit down and eat and drink, come what will!"

So our friends sit down, eat and drink their fill, and stretch their limbs. But lo! the priest's son, who was a cunning fellow, as soon as he saw that the Prince was asleep, got up softly and silently, and hid himself under the bed, saying to himself, "Something is up here." Scarcely had he finished the sentence, when in comes the good housewife, a sorceress, with her daughter.

As soon as the latter sees the young man lying there, she turns to her mother and says :

"Mother, there are men come to our house."

"Mind you keep your counsel," she answers. "Leave them alone, they do but beat the air."

"But why so, mother? May you have no joy with me, unless you tell me."

"Tush, daughter," says she, "there are two of them, and they are after the fairest maiden in the world. But it is to no purpose, that they labour, for in our country is a sea : could the fools but have the wit to go down to the shore, where the pillars are, and dig at the lower one, they would find a bridle : which, if they dropped into the sea, it would become a winged steed, and thus they would be able to mount it to cross the sea."

The priest's son opened his ears as wide as he could; and when they were gone he wakes the Prince, they eat a bit more, and then, "Heart to the front, and feet to the rear," is the word.

When they got down to the shore, the priest's son goes, as the sorceress had said, to the lower pillar and digs. When he had dug someway down, he unearths a bridle (what on earth is the young priest up to!); he dips it in the sea, and lo and behold! out there comes a horse with wings and says, "At your service, master!"

Then the two mounted him, and in a twinkling of an eye, pass over to the country of the Fair One. When they had landed, the horse turns into a bridle again, which they take into the town with them. They inquire of one or two of the people there, and they tell them that this is where the Fair One dwells. Then the Prince smiled, and did not trouble himself to think how they were to accomplish their object. But lo! the priest's son had the wit of a woman, and did business by the bushel. When they had stayed two or three days, and no one so much as gave them a look, he said to his companion one evening, "Well, brother, what's to be done now?" To which the Prince, in a languishing voice, replied, "I'm sure I don't know."

"Well, brother," said his friend, "I have got a plan, that I think of carrying out, and which I want you to listen to, and see whether it meets your views as well. I have come to the conclusion that we should take a cunning artificer into our house, and get him to make us a horse, that a man can get inside of, and to fit it with screws and springs, so that it can be put through all the paces of a live one, and that we should gild it outside, and deck it here and there with a diamonds and other priceless gems, so as to glitter and gleam, and make it a saddle of velvet with golden tassels and a golden bridle, and then let's set it going. Only speech will be lacking to it. And if God grant us success, then shall our enterprise thrive, otherwise we shall 'lose both the eggs and the basket.'" The Prince, who would have said, "very good," to any proposal, on this occasion said it twice, "A very good plan, a very good plan indeed that of yours." So they engage an artificer of the first rank; they pay him handsomely—for they were boiling with impatience—and the rascal makes a horse, which, if anyone had seen when fully caparisoned, he would have said, "Good heavens! give me an extra pair of eyes to look at him!" So beautiful it was. But they had bound the artificer on his oath, not to tell anyone the secret.

Accordingly, next day our good Prince gets into it, and the priest's son starts off with it, and they come right into the capital. The sun was just rising, and the people see a sight which dazzled everyone's eyes. Heart alive! whatever had legs ran to see the wonderful sight, and only to behold the way in which it greeted the populace, curvetting and prancing about like mad! On that day everyone turned out of doors to look at it.

The next day the King also heard of it, and gave orders to bring it to the palace, that the Princess might enjoy the spectacle too. No sooner had they heard this—a thing they scarcely hoped for—than they take it to the palace. The King and the Princess see it, and were almost beside themselves at its beauty. They overwhelmed the priest's son with gracious attentions, and told him to leave it there, and come to fetch it on the morrow, so that they might have a good look at it. What could the young priest do? It was a king's command.

He rises to depart against his will.

All night long no slumber closed his eyes, for he was afraid they would open it: and while it was still quite dark, he runs to the palace and fetches it. When they had reached their little house, he unscrews it, and out comes the Prince, and says, "We got off cheap last night! My heart went pit-a-pat like a clock, until you came to fetch me." "It fared the same with me, you may be sure. But I see we have got as far as the palace, and my fears are passing away. All goes well and prosperously."

The Prince sang aloud for joy, and kept running at all hours in his horse to the palace.

One day the priest's son said to him:

"Eh, brother, how long shall we waste our time to no purpose. This evening you must positively make up your mind to get out of the horse, when they are all asleep—and then let's see what happens "—for the Princess was wont to take the horse into her chamber and loved to look at it.

But do you think the other (who was very timid) could ever make up his mind to any such thing?

So the priest's son for that evening got inside and went to the palace. Ah! but that evening the horse surpassed itself, for the priest's son knew a number of tricks, and made them all split with laughter. At length when the Princess was sleepy she took the darling horse into her room, and played with it again for some time. At length she got into her golden bed, which was filled with roses and other flowers, and just about the time when she was going to close her sweet eyes, out comes the priest's son and stands before her. He was seized with a fit of gasping and could not speak. The Princess, who had not yet gone to sleep, opens and shuts her eyes and looks at him, and makes as though she would call out. Then the priest's son begins with tears in his eyes:

"In the name of God, lady, have pity on poor me! Don't make them kill me without a cause. Ah, light of my eyes! what pains do I suffer for your sake. You must take *some* young man; look at me. I am neither blind nor lame."

At this she stands and considers. She sees before her a handsome youth: she sees him crying like a guileless child. Partly she pities him, and partly she likes him, so she says to herself:

"Suppose now I set up a shouting, what shall I gain by it? While they are coming to catch him, he may kill me first, and end by being killed himself. On the other hand—as I must marry some one—I shall scarce get a better than he."

Then she says to him, "Well and what do you want?"

The heart of the priest's son had recovered itself a little, as it were, and he said to her, "Let us arise, lady, and fly hence!"

"Swear to me," says she, "that you are not taking me away for another."

"Am I such a dolt, my darling, to run this risk for another?" he asked.

But she seemed as though she smelt the trick; however, what could she do? So she gets up and gathers together all her trinkets, and then they make tracks without any one getting scent of them. They run to the house where the Prince was hourly awaiting them, and without their entering at all, all three take to their heels.

Day dawns: the hour came when the Princess was wont to awake. She neither wakes nor stirs.

"Why what's the matter?" says the King. "Why doesn't that fellow come to fetch his horse?" For he always came very early.

At last he seemed to get an inkling of the state of the case, and shouted that they should break open the door. The doors are broken in and what should they see. No princess! no trinkets! only the golden horse lying open on the floor.

"Woe betide me!" shouts the King, "I have lost my only solace! Run to the house of the owner of the horse!"

But in vain is all their trouble! to no purpose all their toil! The bird was flown from the cage.

They muster an armed force, and start in pursuit. But the others were close to the sea, and feared them not.

When the maiden saw so large an army, "See!" said she, "my father is after us, and where shall we go now?"

Then the Prince dips the bridle into the sea and up comes our good horse, and carries them across. Then her father, too, comes to the edge of the shore, but how shall he pass over? Then he utters a curse upon his daughter.

"Daughter, look to it! since you have deserted me and fled, the first night you sleep with your husband may the wall be rent, and a two-headed monster come and eat you up!"

An evil thing is a parent's curse.

Let us now turn to the Prince, who is blithe as a bird on the wing, and wanted at once to be off to his father's. But she was not so well pleased with him. The son of the priest proposed that that they should first go to the castle of the witch, and afterwards proceed to their own country. They could not well do otherwise. They come to the castle, they eat and drink, and then he says to her:

"There is your husband, lady! He is a King's son, and I the son of a priest."

She was like to make a wry face, but she gulped down her vexation and says, " I must put up with him."

Then the two went to sleep and the priest's son again hid himself to listen what the sorceress would say when she saw them. The sorceress comes and straightway her daughter says to her :

" Do you see? they've managed it ! They've got her."

Then the sorceress groaned, and her daughter asked, " Why do you groan, mother?"

" Why do you bother about the business of another ? They will find what they were seeking."

" Nay but tell me, mother darling, tell *me* too, what is the matter. I beg it as a favour."

" Well ! this girl's father invoked the following curse on her : that the first night a monster should appear and eat them both up, and whoever should hear and tell of it should be turned into stone."

" Alas poor creatures ! what woes are in store for them."

Then they ate and departed. When they were gone, the poor priest's son, with a heavy heart, wakes them up, and says to them, " It's time to be off now."

They arise and look at the priest's son. His countenance is fallen. They ask him what's the matter, but he only answers :

" Bless you, brother, I could not sleep, and that has spoilt my humour."

Not to make a long tale of it, when they arrived on the outskirts of the town, they saw the city all in mourning, and asked some of the people they met in the way, why that town is so afflicted : and they replied that the King had an only son, and sent him with the son of a priest on an excursion with great pomp and escort, and at night while the guard was asleep the two lads were lost, and nothing had since been heard of their fate, or whether the wild beasts had devoured them, and on this account the King and the priest no longer desired to live.

Then the others said to them, " Go and bring the tidings that the priest's son and the Prince are both on their way home. and are bringing with them the Fairest Lady in the World."

So they flung up their heels shoulders high, each eager to run first to the king, and get from him the reward of the good news that his son was coming home. When the poor King heard it, he ran out into the road, and met them, and kissed them affectionately, all three of them, and brought them into the palace. The worthy priest went on like a madman. At once mourning was exchanged for mirth. Here was laughing! There dances and songs! and the town from being a hell became a paradise!

As soon as evening fell the King calls lords and priests, and marries his son. They sat for some time at table eating and drinking and merry-making, and afterwards got up to leave the bridal pair to themselves.

But the priest's son said to the Prince, "My brother, you know how hard I have toiled that you might win this success that you *have* won. Now therefore I have a favour to beg of you, which is that I may sleep in the same room with you, and give me your word, that you do not yet consider her as your wife."

What was the Prince to do? awkward as he felt it.

"By all means," he said, "be it as you will."

So the two lie down to sleep on the bed, and the priest's son seats himself in the chair, with his sword in his hand.

When it was just close on midnight, the wall rent in twain, and in flew a monster. Then the priest's son rushed towards the bed with his sword, cut off the monster's heads, and flung him out at the door, without making any mess. But, alas, at the noise the Prince awoke, and seeing him standing over him with drawn sword, supposes that he was going to slay him, and sets up a loud alarm! There is a hubbub in the palace, they run and ask what is the matter. The Prince cries and rends his clothes, and says the priest's son was going to kill him from jealousy. They put every possible pressure on the priest's son to tell them why he approached the bed with his drawn sword, but he was afraid to confess, for he knew he should be turned to marble. The priest and the priest's wife entreat the King's mercy but in vain. Then the priest's son says :

"Oh, King live for ever! Behold now, since I have not slain

your son, banish me to a wilderness. Why do you wish me to perish guiltless?"

"Nay, nay, but you shall tell us!" replies the King.

Then the priest's son could bear it no longer, and said, "I have but one life to lose! What odds does it make? I am only grieved for my father and mother. But you will be sorry afterwards, and the guilt of my undoing be on your heads." So he begins to relate how everything had happened, and then how he heard from the sorceress, that the girl's father had invoked a curse to the effect that on the first night the wall should be rent and a monster should appear to eat them both up.

"And this," he continued, "was why I rushed, sword in hand, and slew it, and cast it forth, and if you don't believe me, come and see for yourselves; but why should I tell you, ingrates that you are.

"But, indeed, the sorceress said one thing more, namely, 'that whoever should overhear and repeat her words, should be turned to stone!'" And forthwith he changed to a marble block, and fell flat on the floor. Then they all began to pull their beards and moustaches, but they might as well have called for rain. When some days had passed the Princess said to the Prince, "That unless he went to the sorceress to learn how to unmarble the priest's son, she would not have him for her husband, but would send him about his business." What was the Prince to do?

He got up and started for the castle, sore against his will, for he was afraid. To make a short story of it, he reaches the castle, and pretends to fall asleep. Again the sorceress and her daughter enter, and behold him again outstretched. "Holloa!" says the maiden, "What does he want now?"

"Eh! don't you remember how I said that whoever overheard and repeated those words of mine, would be turned to stone? There was another hidden, who went and told them, and now this one has come to hear something, so that he may go and restore him. But the favour will not be granted him!"

At last after many entreaties on the part of her daughter, she said, "If he can only bring himself to slay the child which his wife shall bear him upon the marble block, well—but otherwise there is no cure."

The Prince heard it, and when they were gone, he got up and went away too. He came back, and the Princess asked him, "What did she tell you?"

"What shall I say to you, good wife?" he answered, "I heard that the only cure is to kill the child that you shall bear, on the marble block, but I cannot do such a thing."

"I'll do it myself!" says she, "that poor fellow saved us both when the monster would have eaten us, and you would spare a little puling brat?" Her hour comes, she gives birth to a little boy, an angel of a child, and she takes it and slays it on the marble, as if it had been a chicken, such a heart of iron was hers.

Listen there, trickle! trickle! and the marble all melts away, and the priest's son is left behind, and says, "Ah, what a heavy sleep I had, and how lightly am I awaked! Who showed me this kindness?" In a little while he was thoroughly aroused, and sees the child slaughtered; he asks, and learns how all had come about. Then he pitied the little one, that it should have been murdered on his account, and went off to the castle.

Now all this long while the priest's son had loved the daughter of the sorceress, for she was the next in beauty to the Princess, and now he went with the intention of fetching her. So he arrives at the castle, and, on entering it, finds mother and daughter sitting at table. Says he, "Good-day, ladies." "Welcome, young master," says the mother. But the daughter at once fixed her eyes on the ground, as though she were ashamed. Really, from the moment she first saw him, she had set him deep in her heart.

"And why have you come?"

"What shall I say? I love your daughter, and that is the only thing that brings me."

"Ah, you rascal!" says she, "with what wiles do you enslave the world?"

But the sorceress had kept him all along in her eye, and then she said to him, "Well, son-in-law, my daughter just suits you, and I loved you from the first moment you set foot in the castle. Or do you suppose I did not notice you? But take her and depart with my blessing."

And without his saying a word to her, she continues, "Take

too this string, and bind up the child's throat with it, that it may recover."

Then they received the blessing of the old woman and kissed her hand, and took as much treasure as they could carry away from the castle, and departed. They came back to town, and the priest's son went at once and bound up the child's throat with the string, and restored it to life. And at eventide the priest called together his brother priests, and they held the wedding.

Then there was no more sorrow nor suffering, but each lived happily, yes, very happily with his darling wife, and may we live here happier still.

THE GOLDEN CASKET.

(ASTYPALÆA.)

———:o:———

ONCE on a time there was a King and a Queen who had an only son. His father said to him, " My child, you see that we have no other son ; all that I have depends on you. Therefore I desire to see you married, with children growing up to console me before I die, that I may have some joy in my old age, for you are my only hope."

The Prince was by no means willing to be married in spite of all his father could say to him : it simply went in at one ear and out at the other.

About a week later, he said the same thing all over again. He asked him whether he had peradventure, changed his mind : whether he had chosen any one : and promised to give him whomsoever he should take a fancy to.

But you might as well have talked to a stone and expected an answer. His mind was not so easily swayed from its purpose. What was the King to do?

He seeks the intercession of kinswomen : they talk to him again and again ; but without avail. However, it was bruited abroad that in a certain place there dwelt a damsel passing fair : and there was a wager that whomsoever she speaks to. him she shall wed ; but otherwise, whoever is the suitor, they are to slay him.

Well, the fancy seized the Prince that he would essay the wager to win the maiden in question.

Accordingly, one day, when his father was repeating his entreaties, he answered, " Well, Father, as you will have me married, give me that fair maid ? "

" Goodness gracious, my son, bethink you ! " cried the King. " Would that it were in my power! But have not you heard what wagers she lays, and how many fine young fellows she has slain? Do you want her to take your life as well? Why there are princesses and vizier's daughters plentiful as running waters, and not one of them can be found to suit you! But so it is! It's a wise saying, 'Joy to the man, whose name is destined to good luck!'"

"That's all fudge that you are talking, you only want to damp my ardour! I tell you, father, I am not going to marry anyone else. I am off in search of her, and if I get her—good! If not. I will perish for her sake!"

"Alas, my son, how you torture my heart with your impious words! Have you no pity on me, have you no pity on your mother, who had such pains, poor thing, ere she bare you: at your age, big lad as you are! Is that the return we had to look for at your hands, that you should poison and embitter our old age? Alas, what shall we say to you, when you won't listen to your elders, but rush upon your ruin! I only pray, my son, that my evil forebodings may not find fulfilment!"

"Nonsense, nonsense! father. There's no turning me from my purpose."

Then, indeed, the King's eyes were dim with tears, as he wept before him like a little child, and entreated him to have regard to his own welfare: but the other, on his part, was as obstinate as obstinate could be, so his father replied:

"Well, my son, I have said all I could say as your father, and one who pities you, for I would not have a hair of your head come to harm, but you are determined to have your own way. May God have mercy upon you. I offered you a thousand sheep, and you won't so much as take a tail!"

Then he arose and departed, his eyes running rivers of tears.

He went to the Queen, and said to her:

"What shall I tell you, mother dear?

"'Our cruel fate, with ruthless hand, has written the decree.
That winter storms and summer suns alike unkind shall be.'

One son alone was born to us, the light of our eyes, whom everyone was gladdened to behold, and now, even he has got beyond our control, and is going to fling his life away."

" What's the matter ? " says the Queen.

Word for word, he told her, and it was a sad hour when she heard the story. The two mourn together like a pair of ringdoves, and cannot be consoled.

When they see that with all their efforts they can make no advance, they say to one another, "Come, come, what's the good of behaving so childishly in the sight of everyone? He has said it, and he will do it. Only let us give him our blessing, and bid him farewell. 'None can escape his fate.'"

So they summon him on the day that he was preparing to depart, and say to him :

" Darling of our hearts, we sought your welfare, but,

"'Since go thou wilt, then fare thee well, good luck betide each hour,
May roses fair bestrew thy path with many a fragrant flower.
Thou golden eaglet, this alone we crave from thee : wherever
Thy lot be cast, may nothing us from thy remembrance sever.'"

Then the pair fall on his neck, and embrace him fondly, and bedew him with their tears, and can hardly tear themselves away from him. At length they let him go, and tell him he has full power to take what he will along with him.

So he goes and chooses a good horse, takes a little money, and other necessaries, receives the blessing of his father and mother, and, with a " God bless you, dearest parents," is off and away.

The hapless King and Queen plunged themselves in mourning, and so did the whole country.

The Prince journeyed on for several days, till at length he reached a town.

He dismounts, and goes to refresh himself at a little coffeehouse, in order that he may learn something about the place.

There enters a hawker with a beautiful golden casket, and cries it, saying, " This casket for sale ! whoever buys it will rue it : and again, whoever does not buy it, will rue it : the price is a thousand ducats, no more and no less."

Then all who were in the coffee-house turned and looked at the Prince, and he says to himself, " Halloa, here is a start : 'whosoever buys it, shall rue it : and again, whosoever does not buy it shall rue it.' Well, I'll try my luck with it, anyhow, as I see all eyes are turned on me." Then he calls to the man : " Here, sir, what is the price of that casket ? "

" A thousand ducats, neither more nor less."

Then the Prince takes out his purse, and—chink, chink ! he counts a thousand ducats into our good hawker's hands, and takes the casket, and puts it in his pocket, with the words, "Time will show its worth."

He sits a while in the coffee-house, then he gets up and goes, after treating everyone all round, and that twice over. Well, what do you think ? What are you expecting?

To make a short tale of it, he came to the town where the Fair One dwelt. He asks for information, and is told as follows : " My brave lad, have you no care for your young life ? she is a monster without her like. Her heart knows no relenting. Many and many a fine young fellow has she slain, and think you she will spare you ? However, as you are determined, go to the King, and let him tell you what to do."

So the Prince arose, and came to the King, and made his obeisance to him ; and the latter rises and bids him sit down beside him. And at once he took a fancy to him, for he was a fine-looking youth, and very accomplished. He asks him, what is his pleasure ?

And the lad replies, " I have come for your daughter."

" Ah, my son, that's a bad business. She's a witch, and wants to devour the world. I pray you begone ! "

" Nay, nay, nay ! that's out of the question. Let me be slain."

But you see the King himself was weary of so much butchery : and he sware to the Prince, that if she did not speak this time, he would kill her too.

Then the Prince's heart failed him, and he began to doubt of what he had done.

" But," said he (in the words of the proverb) :

" ' Oh ! last and latest thought of mine, why wast thou not my earliest ? '

Farewell, oh King ! "

" Good-bye, my son."

He departs, and goes to a coffee-house, full of thought, and rests his head on his hand.

As he did so, the casket was underneath; it struck against his elbow, and bruised his arm, so that it smarted a good deal. Then said he, " It is good for me to suffer. Did I not hear the hawker say, ' Whoever buys it, will rue it ? ' "

Then the casket answers, and says to him, " Tush, if you did not want me, why did you take me ? "

The Prince was like to lose his wits on hearing the casket talk.

" Don't be astonished," it continued, " I am your salvation. Only listen to what I tell you, and never fear. In the evening you will go to the Fair One's house. As soon as you enter, say, ' Good evening to you,' and see that you put me down somewhere, and afterwards begin to tell as many lies and stories as you can. She, meanwhile, will be sitting aloft by the glass cupboard, she sees you, and you don't see her, and she is as silent as a rock. Then you must say, ' Well, as the Princess doesn't deign to speak to us, won't you speak to us ? ' naming the object on which you have placed me. Then I will begin to talk to you, and you must ask me to tell you a tale, and I shall answer, ' I will, but on your honour, will you pronounce a right judgment thereon ? ' and you must take good care and pronounce one that is altogether wrong. Then she will be indignant, and will speak.

" These, my words, do you obey.
Write on paper what I say."

Then the Prince took heart, and longed for the evening to come. Till night drew on, the day seemed like a year, and when it grew dark—before you could count two—he was with the Princess.

A crowd hurried thither to watch the result from outside, and stood agape. The Prince entered with all politeness, and said, " Good evening, fair lady, light of my eyes ! How are you ? Won't you speak a word to me, the stranger ?

" ' Open thy lips, I pray thee, and speak but two words unto me,
To ease me of these heartfelt pangs, that send their anguish through me.' '

In vain ! not a word was heard.

Alas ! poor Prince,

" Fruitless are all thy strivings, to no purpose all thy pain.
The fish that thou art fishing for, there is no way to gain."

However, while he was scraping and bowing, he managed to place the casket on the shelf, and again began :

"But, in the name of Heaven, is there no one here, not a soul to speak to me ? I shall burst ! I cannot stand it." He makes a cigarette ; he makes another.

No improvement !

"Ha ! what a heartless creature !" they shout from outside. "How many braves have perished, and she does not loose her tongue ! Why a saint under vow of silence would speak !"

"Troth," continues the Prince, "was it not I that used to have any number of men who would cudgel their brains to despair and tax their conversational powers to the utmost, just to amuse me : and now I have come to this nest of savages, to lose my life for nought ! Well spake my sire and my mother ! But since the Lady Princess will not speak with us—will not you, per chance, little shelf, speak a word with us, who are here all alone, and have no one to talk to ? "

"Gladly, master," answers the shelf ; "if I would not speak for your sake, do you think I would for the sake of yonder wretch ? "

"Thanks, little shelf ! "

"What will you have ?—a song, a jest, or a little tale ? "

"Well, to pass the time, let's say—a tale."

"But allow me to say, master, that I shall ask you to deliver a fair judgment thereon ? "

"Now, little shelf, you have spoken a word that has stung me to the quick. Such a Prince as I am, and you tell me to give a fair judgment ? "

"Never mind ! Now for my story.

"The tale begins with wishing your honour good evening. Perish the witch over there," it adds aside.

It was torture to the Princess to behold all this, and to hear such grievous words ; she was like to burst. Meanwhile I am breaking the thread of our story, but no matter.

"Once on a time, Prince, there were three fine young fellows, and all three had the same sweetheart without knowing it, and were also friends of one another. They agree, accordingly, one day to go out into the country to a certain pleasure-garden to enjoy themselves. Do you hear, Prince?"—and he bent himself to listen, like a gipsy's billhook, and his eye was fixed upon it.

"Ah, I forgot! where did we stop? Oh, I believe it was where they were about to go out into the country. Well,—but they wanted a little relish—you understand—so each one sends a lad to his sweetheart to bring him something to eat, without knowing she was the same. Well, do I not tell my story prettily?"

"Charmingly!"

"Now, the good girl had a fowl in the oven, so she takes it and makes three portions of it. Does she know what she is doing?

> "'Beards of hair
> Want comb and care.'

She also takes a little cheese and divides that, too, into three pieces, and a little loaf as well. Then she summons the first lad, takes one of the pieces of fowl, cheese, and bread, wraps it in a handkerchief, ties it up, and gives it to the boy, and goes away. Then she does the same with the next and the next, and the thing is done. The boys—who alone were not the same—take the handkerchiefs, they receive each a trifle for his trouble, and the young men go their way. Then our three friends set off on their journey, each with his handkerchief in his hand. They arrive at the pleasure-garden, whither they were bound. Then, when they had sat down comfortably, they open their handkerchiefs, and what should they behold—but all three the same! 'Well, did I ever?' exclaimed each. Then all three were sore perplexed to get at the bottom of the matter; for they seemed to smell the trick. 'Why, brother,' says the first, 'who is your sweetheart?' Says he, 'So and so.' At once the third exclaims, 'Halloa, that's mine!' 'No,' says the other, 'she's mine.'

"Goodness gracious, what a noise! what words, what shouting! The three young men engage in a deadly quarrel; they come to blows. Here's fine fun! Then one of them, who was more sensible than the others, said to them, 'Come, lads, is it not a shame that we should kill one another for a wench like that? What mischief has possessed us? Some evil eye must have looked at us to-day.' Then the wrath of the others seemed allayed somewhat, and they said, accordingly, 'How shall we settle this business?' 'Is it that which troubles you? Well, my proposal is that each should take off his ring; that we put them underneath this stone, and that then each one should journey forth, and after so many years that we should return hither to the same place, and that we should leave the rings as a pledge that we wait for one another, until we all three meet together, and that then the one who has learnt the best trade should marry her.' 'A good plan that!' say they, and leave their rings and go. So away they went, and each of them learnt a trade: and after three years' space the three meet again in the same place. 'Thank God!' say they, 'that we have met again. Now let us see what we have been about.' Says one, 'I, my lads, have become a famous astrologer, and can tell all about everything.' 'Bravo! well done!' say the rest. The second says, 'I have become an eminent doctor, and can raise the very dead!' Says the third. 'I, in my turn, have learnt to run swifter than the wind: and wherever I wish to be, there I am in a trice.' (Mercy on us, what clever devils! it makes one's hair stand on end!) Then the three say, 'We are well: but come, astrologer, look how fares it with our sweetheart?' Then the astrologer goes and gazes at her star, and trembles, and is like to fall ('For,' says he, 'some one's light is being quenched—he or she is dying!') 'Halloa, you fellows!' he shouts, 'she is at her last gasp!' 'Come, doctor!' they cry, 'physic, for God's sake, quick!' The doctor gathers a few herbs, and makes the medicine. 'Now you, who can go so quick, run for your life!' In a minute he arrives, pours the medicine down her mouth, and her soul, which had by this time reached her teeth, went down her throat again.

"Bless me, what a lot I know! Wasn't that a fine story? Now it's your turn to tell me (for I fain would know) which of the three ought to marry her? and I wish you joy of your answer."

He pretends to reflect, and says at length, "Which should marry her? Which should marry her? Why the astrologer should marry her!"

Then the Princess was in such a torment of indignation, that she uttered such shrieks as made the windows shake. It was, "Spill egg, or burst!"

"I have you now!" says the Prince.

"I wish you joy of your just judgment, Sir Prince!" says she.

" What are you thinking of? Why, if it had not been for that swift runner, of what avail would have been the astrology and the medicine? So let the last one take her!" And she was silent again.

Then you might have heard the clap! clap! clap! of many hands. "The Princess has spoken!" They run to the King. On hearing the news, the King distributed bounties wholesale, and cried, "Glory be to God for changing her mind!"

Then the Prince, on his part, secretly takes away the casket, and with the words, "That scores one for us!" departs,—for the wager was to make her speak three times. This was the condition of success. The Prince goes to the King, who embraces him, and says, "Henceforth you are my son. As she has spoken the first time, the others will follow of themselves." And now there was nothing but rejoicings and carousals. Well, what next? The second evening came; but now he had more courage, and said again, "Good evening to you!" and much else, as on the first occasion, and a great deal more beside. But I forgot to tell you one curious circumstance. When they were all gone, and the Princess was left alone, she got up and descended from her perch, and was in such a passion that the very stones were an offence to her. She went to the shelf, and said to it, "Come, little shelf, won't you speak to me?" But why expect words from wood? Then she nearly choked with passion. "You precious torment! I have had you all these years, and I never remember to have heard you speak a single word to please me; and that fellow that you only saw last night, with him you began to chatter!—take that for your pains, with my compliments." And smash! smash! she breaks the shelf into a thousand splinters, and all the things upon it are sent about their business. You see it was enough to put a saint into a fury. Confusion seize upon her, the silly wench!

On that evening he placed the casket on a chair, and he spoke and spoke again, for his tongue was bolder than before. "Talk! talk!" said he. "Ah, I shall burst with anger again this evening. I have no company. Last night I had my little shelf; but this evening I see it nowhere. Has that turned against me, too?"

" 'All wish me ill! the stocks and stones their human malice aiding,
And if I lean against a tree, the leaves do fall a fading.'

Well, the 'Princess will speak to me no more! But you, my little chair, have not you a word to say to me?"

" Right gladly, Master, I am at your service. What sort of talk do you wish me to begin with you? Shall I tell you a tale to console you, so that the night may pass somewhat more quickly? I will do so, Prince, but I desire a just decision on what I tell you."

" It's too bad to talk to me in that way. I am not a mere child without sense. I am a full-grown Prince, and shall I not give you a just judgment? "'

" Ah, pardon me, and let me begin my story. My story begins by wishing you good evening, my pretty master. Once on a time there were three companions, each of a different calling, One was a monk, one was a carpenter, and one was a tailor. They decided on leaving that country, as they could not get on there any longer, and on going to another place, where there might be a demand for their services. So our good friends arose, and set off for the town in question. They walked all that day, and at evening came to a farm. They decided that they must stay there for that night and would go forward in pursuit of their business on the following morning. But you see they were afraid of all going to sleep at once, for in those parts robbers were known to be about, and fears prevailed all around. What then should they do? They determined to cast lots, and that each should watch in his turn, while the other two slept. The lots are cast, and the first falls on the carpenter. The monk and the 'tailor slept, and the carpenter kept watch. He sat and sat, but soon began to nod. In order to enliven himself and to frighten the tailor, whose turn came next, he took a block of wood which was near the sheep-fold, got his tools, and carved it into the figure of a maiden, and set it up in front of the fold. When his hour was past, he woke the tailor, saying 'Wake up you, and watch a bit.' So he lay down himself, and the tailor got up. Some time passed before he saw anything in particular. At last, when his eyes were thoroughly opened, he turned and beheld the figure. At first he thought, in his terror, that the robbers were there, and shouted, ' To arms! to arms, lads! They have come to attack us!' But he sees that it does not move from its place, and takes courage.

"Then he throws a stone, which struck as though upon wood, which it really was. 'A nice trick that devil of a carpenter has played me, and I was near making a fine mess of it in my fear. However, he has made this figure, and now what shall *I* do?' Then he opened his bag and took out some of the materials and instruments of his trade, and made a dress for the figure, and clothed it, so that if you had seen it, you would have said it was alive.

"But you see, it was not able to speak.

"By the time he had done all this, his time had passed, and he woke up the monk.

"The poor monk gets up, and sees in the sheep-fold a girl in full array, only one thing was wanting to her, and that was life.

"Now the monk understood this, and he put up a prayer to God out of a pure heart. God heard him, and granted his request. Now attend! In the morning, the other two get up, and the three fight together as to who had the first claim to her.

"The carpenter said, 'She belongs to me, because she was a wooden block, and I made her what she is.'

"The tailor said, 'Nay, but she belongs to me, because I spent so much on clothing her, who else would be naked.'

"Finally, the monk begins to talk like a divine, 'God bless you, my sons, will you not leave her to me, who have no one, and am all by myself? You have your wives, your children, all joy to you with them! but whom have I?'

"They clamour, and refuse to hear him.

"I want, therefore, to learn which of them ought by right to take her?"

"Bah! such a trifle need not puzzle your head! The poor tailor ought to have her, for he broke his needle, and made his fingers sore in sewing her clothes together."

At hearing this again, the Princess calls out, "I want to speak once more! For I can't understand such absurdity. Alas, for you, young man! I am sorry for the honour of your name, but you don't seem to know how many days there are in a year! Why look at the absurdity of the thing! While he doesn't know the evil things his destiny has in store for him, he speaks big boastful words : but that's a wise saying :

> " ' Where you hear of many cherries,
> Hold small baskets for the berries.'

[*i.e.* Much cry, little wool.]

" Only I beg you will not come near me again to vex my soul with any more of your nonsense."

Then he says to her, " Since your ladyship has spoken, I am content."

So he puts the casket in his bosom and—catch him if you can —he's off in a jiffey to the King. Our fair damsel comes down from her perch : and falls to fighting with the chair until she has reduced it to atoms. Ah, well, let's see what happens on the following evening ; as everything now depends on that, lest we lose all our labour now, and the fruits of our labour in the past. From early morn she washes herself, combs her hair, puts on her best attire, and when evening was come—

> " Tree of beauty, cypress tree, accept me for your peer ! "

Again he says, " Good evening to you, Princess ! Peradventure you are still angry with me from last evening. I made a mistake, but afterwards I recognised it myself, so pray forgive me for offending you. Only speak to me one word, to heal my wounded heart. Nay, wait a bit. It is as though I understood to-night, how to turn my very soul inside out. What shall I say to my fate that wrote so many bitter things against me ! But here is that will tell me."

He places the casket on the candle-stick and as he poured forth these complaints the candle-stick replied, " Patience, Prince ! "

> " ' What patience, patience ever more ? how long is that to be ?
> Behold the work of patience, what it has done to me ! ' "

answers the Prince.

" Never mind her up there," it replies, " and I will sing and dance for you the live-long night, and don't trouble yourself four rushes about yonder witch, only tell me what I can do for you."

" What shall I say ? Will you tell me a tale to pass the night away ? "

" As you like master, but I want you to pass a just judgment on it."

" Never fear ! "

" Well then : once on a time (may the Holy Virgin protect you, Prince) there was a King and a Queen. They had a daughter, whom they gave to a foster mother to bring it up in a castle. The girl grew up, and one day, when her wet-nurse was combing her hair, she finds a lady-bird. Do you suppose such as she would know a ladybird when they saw it ?

" ' What's that ? ' says she ? when the nurse showed it her.

" ' Why my darling it's a lady-bird.'

" ' Let's keep it, mama, to see if it will grow very large.'

" ' Oh, they don't grow child ! '

" ' Well but I insist that you put it in that vessel that we may see what it comes to.'

" So they put it in and kept it, and lo and behold it got so big it filled the whole jug, and they put in a larger one ; then into a cask--and to make a short tale of a long one—it grew into an ox. Then they thought it was time to slaughter it and to preserve its skin, so that no one would know what it was. They call a butcher and say to him :

" ' Slay this beast for us, and skin it, and throw the remains away.'

" So he slaughters it and skins it without knowing what manner of beast it was. They pay him off, and he goes about his business. They pickle, dry and preserve the skin. Some years passed away, and the maiden was of age to marry. But the Devil put it into her head that she would not marry, and in order that her father might not bother her every day with proposals, she tells him that she has a skin, and whoever can find out what animal it belonged to, him she will marry : otherwise he must lose his head.

" ' So be it,' said he.

" For he supposed that would be the easiest thing in the world, and how was he to know what was in the wind ? So the King issues a proclamation, ' Whoever shall be found to guess my

daughter's riddle " (a similar case to yours and that of this lady
now, who arches her neck like a gipsy's billhook !) ; but it remained impossible for any one to guess it, and many and many
were slain daily, princes and sons of viziers. Neither God nor the
Devil desired such bloodshed for the sake of one woman : but
the Devil took the shape of a handsome young fellow, and he
straightway goes and sues for the hand of the maiden ; a youth
so fair to look on that whoever beheld him, his eyes would be
enchained by his beauty.

" The King sees him, the Queen sees him, the nurse sees him.

" ' Oh, my eyes,' they cry, ' what a beautiful youth ! Would that
he might guess the riddle, and wed our maiden, that she might
live with him to a good old age ! '

" Never fear but he will succeed. You know they say, ' God
judges in His own good time ! ' And now she has shed such
torrents of blood—is it ever to be so ? ' What a man sows, that
shall he reap.' (These sayings don't belong to the story, but are
proverbs of my own, for I have seen and known their truth). So
the handsome youth goes, with all gravity, and asks what the
riddle is. A fluttering at the heart seized the Princess lest he
guess it. Our friend says at once, ' Bah ! why that's the skin of
a lady-bird ! ' "

" Bravo ! bravo ! he has guessed it ! " assents the Princess.

" The very same evening they make ready to marry them.
They ate, they drank, they caroused ; the hour for bed-time came.
The Princess went to bed, while he turned to a black negro, and
slept in the further part of the room, without touching her with
his little finger.

" The greater part of the Princess' blood had congealed from
fright before daylight broke. When the dawn had come, he again
became what he was before, and the girl, though overwhelmed
with grief, said nothing to her father, in order to see how matters
would turn out ; but when she sees how next night things were
the same, and worse, ' Eh !' said she to herself, ' this can
neither be eaten nor chewed ; ' and she runs to her father, and
tells him how matters stand, and begs him to call her husband,
and inquire into the case.

" So the King calls him, and asks him how it is ; and he answers that he is under a curse pronounced on him by his father, and hence his affliction; he begged him to leave him the Princess, that she might go and find his father, and win his blessing, that so he might be delivered from the plague, after which he would return. Then he obtains the Princess: the King gives him a body-guard into the bargain, and he takes his leave. As they were journeying in a wilderness, he changes into a demon, and says, 'Wife, I am hungry!' and straightway he gobbles up all the food they had. They go further, and again he cries, 'Wife, I am hungry!' and he gobbles up all the men of their escort, along with their horses, and only leaves his wife. Then he brought her to a place, where he lifted up a marble slab, and underneath there was a cave, and he put her inside, and covered her up. Alas, unhappy Princess, what sights were there to see! She sees slain beasts, she sees the flesh of men, she sees things that filled her soul with horror. Afterwards the monster comes and lifts the marble slab, and comes in and gives her human flesh to eat, and turns into a snake, and winds himself round her from her foot up to her head, and puts out his tongue, and thrusts it into her mouth, and sucks her blood. When the night was past he leaves her again, and departs.

"But she was at death's door. Now when she left the palace she had taken with her, as a token of her mother's blessing, two ring-doves, which she carried in her bosom; and nothing else remained to her for her solace but these two ring-doves; and she thought to take a piece of paper, and write a letter to her mother, telling her the state of the case, and to tie it to the claw of one of the ring-doves, and let it go when the monster should leave, and if he did not discover it, hoped that something might turn up. So she takes the piece of paper, and ties it to its claw, and lets it go away along with the monster: the poor dove tries to fly out as he lifts the marble, but he perceives it, and swallows the bird whole. The next day she lets the other bird go. That one, by her mother's blessing, escaped, as luck would have it, and flew, and flew, and flew, and perched at the window of the Princess' castle.

"Then her mother sees it, and says, 'Halloa! that is my daughter's dove that has come back! Run and bring it in.' It was as though the poor thing understood, for, instead of flying away, it remained still, and they catch it, and bring it to the Queen. She kissed it fondly, and caressed it, and asked it, 'How fares your mistress?' As she was caressing and stroking it, she sees the paper wrapped round its claw : she unties it, and what does she read? Lamentation and woe! Her cry went down to earth, and up to heaven. The King hastens to her side. 'What's the matter? what's the matter?' says he, and she gives him the paper, and weeps, and groans, 'Ah, my daughter, my daughter! in what a sad plight art thou! and who shall rescue thee?'

" Forthwith a proclamation goes forth into the town, that whosoever shall be able to bring the King his daughter, shall take her to wife. But no one can be heard of. There is no room here for deception! Lamentation and wailing resound through all the town. There was there a certain poor old dame, and she had seven sons, and, verily, every one of them was a hero. You must know they had been absent for seven years, and, by good fortune, they chanced to come home that same year. They see the whole place in mourning, and do not know the reason. They ask two or three people, 'My friends, what's the matter here?' and learn the state of affairs. They go home, and their first word was that their mother must go to the King, and tell him her sons are equal to the task of bringing him back his daughter. 'My dear children,' says their mother, 'you have been all these years away from me, and the grief of your absence consumed me : and scarcely have you come, when you want to go away again. It is no proper business for you, that you are after. And she, they say, is in a horrid place, where not even a gnat can enter.' They answer her, 'We told you to go to the King, and are you still sitting there?' What could the poor woman do? Willing, or unwilling, she goes to the King and tells him. The King was delighted to hear such good news, and loaded her with handsome gifts, and told her that if God grants them success, and they get back his daughter, one of them shall have her to wife, and the others shall share the half of his kingdom ; and whatever they require for their journey, let them come and ask for it. She goes and tells her sons, and they cannot be off soon enough. Now you must understand that at the time of their absence they had not remained idle, like some people, but each had learned a magic art, and this was why they now felt no concern. Here is a list of their accomplishments. One had learnt to put his ear to the ground and find out what was taking place in the under world. The next could lift such a load with his hands, that if even the earth had but a brass handle, he could raise it. The third was so clever and dexterous that he could strip a man asleep without his being aware of it. The fourth had such a pair of shoulders that whatever weight you put upon them he did not feel it. Another had the art of striking his hand upon the earth, so as to make an iron castle spring up, which did not care even for thunderbolts. Another, again, could aim at an object no bigger than a midge upon the devil's thigh, and bring it down.—I'm sure I don't know how many we have now,—will you count them, Prince? That's a wise saying, 'I give the blows, and you count them,' for there's no knowing what mistakes may happen any hour. But I fancy there is yet one left, yes,—the last, who, if anything fell from the sky, and he opened his arms, it would tumble into them. He made it come to him, like that thing that draws iron to itself, the name of which I don't remember. My word, what a devil's brood! What arts they had picked up among them! Bravo, old dame's sons!

"Well, when they had set out on their journey, they said to the one that could overhear the doings of the under world, 'Find out where we are going, so that we may not journey in the dark ; but may arrive an hour in advance, lest the hare give us the slip, and we lose all the fun!'

"'We are going on all right, but we have not gone far enough yet.'

"So they journey on and on, and again they ask, 'Now have another look!'

"'Eh, my lads, we are getting near,' said he : 'it's just behind that mountain there.' Forward, forward! Our young heroes behold the marble slab which was over the cave, and—Heaven preserve us—it was two or three times the size of our house. When they arrived at the spot, they cried, 'Now you who lift the weights—raise up that marble slab!'

" So he took it up by a brass ring which was attached to it and lifted it clean off, but very softly, so that they might not hear him down below.

" Then the one who heard what was doing in the under world said, that the monster was at present a snake, and was coiled round the maiden and sucking her blood with its tongue.

" Then they said, ' Ho ! you, who cannot be seen ; quick, get you down.'

" So he went down below, took the serpent by his tail, and little by little he uncoiled it from her body, without being perceived ; but the girl was by this time half dead. Then he comes up and says, ' She is now ready for raising,' and at once the one who lifted heavy weights went down, and took her on his shoulders, and made off with all haste. The day dawns, and then the snake sees what has happened. ' Ha ! you dogs !' he shouts ; ' the old woman's sons have carried her off !'

" For it seems he knew that they were his fated foes : and straightway he changes to a cloud, and pursues them. Then the long-eared one gets wind of his coming, and says, ' Oho my lads ! he is awake and after us !' Scarcely had he uttered the word when the black cloud loomed in sight. Then they cry, ' Ho ! you who can rear a tower with a clap of your hands, quick, or we have lost her !' In a moment the fine fellow claps down his hand, and a tower rose which was a terror to behold. They all went into it : and there came the cloud, and made a noise and an uproar, that shook the tower to its base, but what did they care ? By this time all the young heroes were wearied out, and wished to take a little nap. to rest themselves. So they said to the maiden, ' You see we are going to lie down to sleep. Be well on your guard, and don't look out at the window, or woe betide you ! It will be the worse for you.'

" It was as though they had said to her, ' As soon as we are gone to sleep, mind you look out at the window,' for the foul fiend, when he had tried every artifice and could accomplish nothing, changed to an old woman, with a brood of golden birds, and kept casting pearls to them, which they ate, and made such sweet music it was ravishing to hear.

" Then had it been myself, I must have had a peep, to say

nothing of the Princess; who had been so many days in hell, and longed to have a look at the world. But why do they call them devils? Because with their arts they deceive the world. The poor girl goes to peep out, and see! The black cloud seizes her, and mounts up aloft as high as it can. Then the young braves wake up, they seek the maiden. Where is she? She can nowhere be seen or heard. The tower builder strikes on the floor, the tower vanishes: they look this way, they look that—not a sign of her. Then they turn their eyes aloft, and behold our friend the fiend carrying the girl up into the clouds, at such a height that he now looked about the size of an onion. They shout, ' Ho there! you who have a good aim! Quick, or we shall lose them.' But he answers, ' Let them alone, let them get a bit further.' They rose higher still, till they were scarcely seen at all, and then he shoots his arrow, and it goes and strikes the monster right in the breast just where the heart is, and in a moment they see them come tumbling down together. Then the other one opens his arms, and in a little while afterwards down falls the fiend as well, and is dashed to pieces, and so they, too, were rescued from his clutches. Then they cheer up the maiden and bring her to her father. Now then, I prithee, tell me, master, who has a right to marry the maiden?"

He thought and thought and at length he said, " It is right that he should take her who carried her such a way."

At hearing this again the Princess took fire and was in a burning rage. Then she said, "Now that is too bad! I am doomed to lose my life for this brat of a foreign woman! Good sir, didn't I tell you not to presume to show your face again in my presence to set my heart aflame? Why do you come and drivel away in here, and spoil other people's humour, for I'm blessed if you know a hen's tail from its beak!"

" All right, my lady, now the whole thing is over."

And wherever you went you heard nothing else but, "The Princess has spoken." Let the Prince thank his casket for his luck, for it was that which made a man of him. Then the King orders his daughter to wash herself, and comb herself, and put on her best attire, for at eventide he would have her married. So the maiden made ready, and in the evening he married her to the

Prince, and there was laughter and joy and grand carousal. A few days later the Prince asks leave to go and see his father and mother, to comfort them in their grief and anguish. "By all means," says his father-in-law, "and take your wife with you." So the Prince sets off with the Princess, and they come to his father. When the poor unhappy parents saw their son coming whom they had long given up for lost, they were almost crazy with joy. Then the King took off his crown and put it on his son's head, and the mother did the same to the daughter, and henceforward, free from torment and mishap they lived a right merry life; and may we live a better one still, for neither I nor you were there to know whether it was true.

THE CUNNING OLD MAN.

———— :0: ————

ONCE on a time there was an old man and an old woman, and they had no son.

They were good managers : they had, in fact, vineyards, fields, cattle, and, in short, were well provided with everything.

When the old man was very aged, and could no longer manage his stock, they made up their minds to sell it, in order to live comfortably in their declining years. So they take and sell everything and leave only one pretty heifer, which the old woman wanted to cheer her, since they had no other company. So the good dame kept the heifer for some time, and fed it, and gave it to drink, as though it were her child. At length, when it had grown big, and she was tired of it, she says to her husband :

" You had better find a customer for the cow, for I have had enough of it."

" Whom am I to find," says he. " Since you wish to sell it, you had better take it yourself, next Sunday morning, and bring it to the village, where the people are gathered together, and find a market for it."

The old man's advice was good, so she acted upon it accordingly. Right early on the Sunday morning the good dame takes the cow and drives it to the village. As she was driving it along, the tithe-takers of the place saw her, and agreed among themselves to cheat the old woman, and get the cow at the price of a goat. So they get up and go to the church. The old dame also takes the cow and goes to the church door, and waits till the people come out, that she may sell it. The three tithe-takers, having concerted their plans to cheat the old woman, the first of them comes out, and says to her :

" Good dame, what say you? How much do you want for that goat?"

" Good sir," quoth she, " what do you mean, don't you see that this is no goat, but a cow : or are your eyes so dazed that you cannot see well ? "

" My dear good woman," says he, " pray come to your right senses, and don't talk such nonsense, unless you want people to laugh at you. I'll give you thirty piastres, and you give me the goat."

" Kind sir, as you are a Christian, do not tease me thus," she answers.

But before she had gone further, out comes the second. He also addresses her in the same way :

" Well, my good woman, will you let me have that goat ? "

The old woman, who was more or less chuckle-headed, took a good long look at the cow, to see whether it really was a goat after all.

" My good sir," says she, " that's a cow, and you call it a goat."

" Nonsense," says he, " you're joking."

" And how much will you give me for it ? " says the old woman.

" How much will I give ? " he replied. " Well, for your sake, I don't mind saying twenty-five piastres. You see it is rather past its prime, old lady."

" Nay, that will never do," says she, " why my husband would be the death of me : yonder fellow, who is waiting over there, offered me thirty, and you offer me twenty-five."

" Well, you are welcome to keep it, good dame," said he, and went and sat down beside the other, and the two waited for their companion. In a short while he, too, came out. But the poor old woman, hearing first one and then another say it was a goat, almost began to believe it must be so. Then the third rogue also began :

" Good day to you, mother, what are you sitting here for ? Do you want to sell that goat of yours ? "

Ah, then the old woman believed outright, and simply said :

" I do, my son."

" Well, I'll give you twenty piastres. Can I have it ? "

Says the old woman to herself, " If I ask too much, I shan't get anything at all."   So at length she says :

" Why the first one offered me thirty, and you offer me twenty. Come, my good man, do you take it for thirty."

And so they get over the old woman, and take her cow at the price of a goat.

Off goes the old woman to her husband, and gives him the thirty piastres, and says :

" Eh, husband, only think what a laughing stock I've made of myself to-day.   Why I was the butt of all the people.   As I was going to the village, my cow turned out a goat, and there was I going and trying to cheat people by selling it for a cow, when it was a goat all the while."

At that hearing, the old man kindled with anger, and said to her :

" Heart alive, wife, who told you it was a goat ? "

" So-and-so," she replies ; " and what's more, they've bought it."

" Oh, indeed ! " said the old man.   " Never mind, wife. but I'll have it out of them yet."

So the next day our old friend goes and finds another farmer, and buys of him a venerable donkey, some hundred years old, and takes and sticks three gold and three silver coins under his tail, and drives him to the village—to the very place where the rascals lived.   When they see the old man too, they cluster about him like so many flies, thinking they have found another windfall, and that here is a fine opportunity for cheating the old man. But the old man was a match for a thousand like them : so when they address him with : " Well, old man, do you want to sell that donkey ? " he ·replies, " Why, my lads, I scarcely know what to say.   I never meant to sell that donkey at all, for there's not another like it to be bought for love or money.   But, after all. I've made my fortune out of it.   Live and let live, say I."

" But why can't you buy its like ? "

"Well, it does not look a high-bred animal, I admit.   But what can you want more of it, when it keeps dropping ducats ? "

" What ! you don't say so, old man.   Has it really that advantage ? "

"I should rather think so," he replied, "and, if you don't believe me, wait and see."

And therewith he began to belabour the wretched ass with his stick. The poor beast got so uncomfortable and restless with such a dose of cudgelling that it lifted its tail, and down comes a ducat; and a little while afterwards, down comes a dollar, and so on, till he had dropped all that the old man had put there. At length the rogues cried out :

"Enough ! enough ! that will do ! we believe you, old man !" and they winked at each other, as much as to say, "Now we have found our fortune."

"Come now, old man," they said, "what do you want for it ? We'll give you five thousand piastres."

Then he answered, "What are you talking of ? Go about your business. Didn't I say it wasn't for sale ?" And he makes as though he would go on.

"Don't go away," say they: "we'll give you ten—fifteen thousand, come !"

In the end he palms it off on them for twenty thousand piastres.

"And what do you give it to eat, old man ?" they ask him.

"What do I give it to eat ?" says he. "I did not feed it extra well. I used to give it a bit of chaff, and a drop of water. Now do you take it, shut it up in the stable, put plenty of food and water before it, and in three days you may go and find the stable well nigh full."

So he takes his tidy little sum of piastres, and goes back to his old wife.

Then our fine fellows walk off with the donkey, and shut it up, as the old man told them, in a stable, and instead of giving it chaff they give it barley, so that it may produce the more abundantly ; set water before it, and leave it. The good donkey fastened on the barley, and ate and ate as much as ever he could, for he was famished with hunger ; he drank water on the top of that, so that the barley swelled, and the donkey burst. When the three days were passed, the tithe-takers met together. And each one of them takes a bag to fill it with the money. They come to the

stable and turn the key in the lock, and push against the door ;
but it won't open.

" Eh, my lads !" cry they to one another, " it seems he has
made a sight of money. Why, the door won't open." How
should they know that the donkey was dead on the other side,
with his feet stretched out towards the door, and that was why it
would not open ? After a long time they break it open, and,
instead of finding the money they expected, they find the donkey
dead. Then they tore their hair, and cried, " Oh, the rascally old
wretch, a fine trick he has played us !" and they ran to find the
old man.

Now the old fellow was well aware that all this would follow,
and so what do you think he did ? He went and bought two
hares as like as like could be, and the next day he said to his
wife :

" Good wife ! look you ; mind you cook me such and such
things for dinner to-day, and when I come with my guests I shall
say to you, 'Wife, have you cooked me anything to-day ? ' and
you must answer, ' Yes, I've cooked what you sent me word by
the hare that I was to cook.' "

Then he takes one of the hares and a pipe, and goes into the
village, and sits down in a tavern and begins to smoke his pipe.

It chanced that the tithe-takers passed by and saw him inside.
Then they enter and sit down near him, and say to him :

" Old man, do you know the donkey is dead, and now we don't
know what to do ? "

The old man, cunning fellow that he was, no sooner heard that
the donkey was dead, than he began to weep and wail, and cry
and groan. " Alas ! my donkey, why did I sell you ? You who
made a man of me, and one who sports a pipe and all ! And
I never kept you to provide for my old age ! "

At this they were much astonished. " Why, old man ! " said
they, " why do you go on like that ? We have lost our very life's
blood, and we don't weep like you ! "

" And what did you give it to eat ? " he asked them.

" Well, if you must know, old man, we gave it a bit of barley."

" Ah, murderers ! " he cried, " you have killed my poor beast ! "

And the long and the short of it is, that he so bamboozled

them that they had to console *him*. In a while he says to the hare :

"Do you think you could go to the house, and tell your mother to cook so and so for dinner, for I am going to entertain some friends to-day ? "

And he let the hare run. Our friend, the hare, no sooner got loose than it took to the hills, and, for what I know, is running still. Then the tithe-takers were much exercised in mind, and wanted to go to the house, to see if the hare really went to take the message home. The old man guessed what was in their thoughts. and said to them :

"If you like, you may come to my house to-day, and have a bit of something, and comfort my old. woman when she hears about the donkey."

"Gladly, father," they replied, and rose and came to the old man's house.

As soon as they arrived there, the old man called out :

"Have you got anything for dinner to-day, wife ?"

"I have cooked what you sent word by the hare I was to cook," she answered.

And she put on the table the dishes that the old man had told the hare to order.

They see also the other hare. Then they begin whispering together about asking the old man to sell them the hare.

"That's out of the question !" cried the old man ; "I've been made a fool of once, and sold you the donkey, and you've killed it for me."

When the old woman heard that the donkey was dead, she wept and beat her breast, as the old man had instructed her to do.

"What, and give you my hare too, the only comfort left me ! No, no, husband, it cannot be !" cried the old woman.

But they besieged the old man with entreaties. "Oh, give it us, pray give it us ! You shall have thousands on thousands of piastres for it, if only we may have the chance of recovering our loss." When the old woman heard that they were willing to give her husband ten thousand piastres, she said :

"Ah well, let them have it, husband, as they want it so much ; and let us think we never had it."

Then they pay him ten thousand piastres, and take the hare and go. On the way, one of them observed, "I will now send it to my wife, and tell it to order her to cook me such and such dishes, and if you choose, send word by it at the same time to your wives." So the second said, "Let it go to my wife also, and tell her so and so;" and the third said, "Well, it may say so and so to my wife as well." Then they said to the hare, "Well, did you hear what we told you?"

The hare shook its ears, and they supposed it meant to say, "Yes!" and let it go, and it took to the hills, and they cried, "Eh, look at it! It's not going straight to the village. It wants to take a turn first!"

Never fear but the old man will make you open your eyes!

Not to make too long a tale of it, the day passed, and in the evening each goes home.

"Well wife," says the first, "did the hare come and tell you to cook?"

When his wife heard him say that, she exclaimed, "Mercy on us, husband, what are you thinking of? Are you mad?" and she crossed herself. "Never a hare, nor a leveret did I see."

The same thing happened to the other two.

The first went to the house of the second one. "Well," said he, "did the hare come to your house?"

"Not a bit of it," he answered, "and I've been abusing my wife."

So he went to the third. The same tale!

"Eh, my lads," they say to each other, "it's too late to-night, but early to-morrow morning we will meet and go together to look up the old man."

Till the next day dawned they had a hard time of it, for not one of them could sleep for vexation ; and, as soon as the first streak of light appeared, they got up and went to visit the old man. But the evening before the old man had said to his wife, "Good wife, those fellows will be sure to come to-morrow to look after the hare. Now I am going to tie a bladder filled with blood round your neck, and when they come, I shall pretend to be in a passion, and cut the bladder so as to spill the blood, and you must tumble down and not stir a limb, but pretend to be dead ; and when I play the flute to you, you must get up again."

So early in the morning our friends came to the old man's house, and angrily accosted him as follows :

" The hare you gave us never went home when we sent it, and we have only lost it for our pains."

" Ah," answered the old man, " my child was vexed with me, I suppose, and took to the hills : and it's all the fault of that old wife of mine;" and he got up, and. drew his knife, and plunged it into the bladder, and out spurted a quantity of blood, and the old woman fell flat on the floor, and turned up her toes.

At this dreadful sight they were dumbfounded. At length they said to the old man :

" Old man, old man ! have you no fear of God before your eyes, to do such a murderous deed ? "

" What, does that shock you ? " said he, and he takes his flute, and, at the first note, the old woman gets up again. When they saw her get up, they were astounded indeed, and said to the old man :

" Good father, will you let us have that flute ? We'll give you thirty thousand piastres for it."

" Stuff and nonsense ! Do you think I am going to let you have it, when I can kill my wife whenever I like, and raise her to life again with it ? "

Says one of them, " Nay, but you must give it to us."

And, to be short, he gives them the flute as well, and they take their departure. As they walked along, they said to one another, "Well, we've bamboozled the old man, and now we'll go, wake the dead with our flute, and become famous men."

So they come to the village, and the first one takes the flute; and no sooner has he entered his house than he picks a quarrel with his wife, and then and there whips out his knife, and without a moment's hesitation, he gives a playful stab in the breast and stretches her dead on the floor. Then he takes his flute, and plays and plays, but in vain : so he weeps and beats his brow, because he has killed his wife. Then he thinks to himself, "If I tell them my wife did not come to life again, they will not kill theirs, and they will take me for a madman. Nay, let them have the same experience as myself." So he went and found number two, and put a bright face on it: and the other asks him, "Well, what success had you?"

"Good, brother," says he, "no sooner did I play, than she stood bolt upright at once."

Then the other seizes it, and goes to his wife, and, without any provocation, finds some fault with her, and takes out his knife, and kills her. Then he plays the flute, but he might as well have piped to the stones, "Alas, what have I done?" says he to himself, "perhaps I don't know how to play it. How was it the other told me he raised his wife? However, I had better say nothing now, and afterwards I will get one of them to bring my wife to life again." And so he brought it to the other, and he treated his wife in the same way. And then they rush like madmen, the one to the other, begging one another to restore their wives to life; and they wept and bewailed the fate that had befallen them, that they could not let well alone, but must go and kill their wives. Then they went to the Cadi, and accused the old man of having caused them this trouble. The Cadi summons the old man.

"Old man," says he, "what is this business you have been doing?"

Then the old man replied, "Cadi, even as they cheated my wife, and took from her her cow at the price of a goat, even so have I cheated them. They should have kept their eyes well opened!"

So our clever old man got the best of the bargain, and gave our friends, the tithe-takers, a good dressing. And he lived with his old woman a right merry life, and may we live a merrier still.

"Set a thief to catch a thief."

THE SHOEMAKER AND THE PRINCESS.

(ASTYPALÆA.)

——— :o: ———

ONCE on a time there was a shoemaker, who, by following his trade, managed to get rich. He built houses and stores ; he had man-servants and maid-servants, and lived in style. But later on he had three daughters, and they wasted his substance in riotous living, and in a few years devoured all their father's possessions, which he had amassed with the sweat of his brow, until he was forced to go half shod, and, from being a master shoemaker, he became a cobbler who was glad to earn a penny to feed his family withal. One day there came by a Jew and asked him to mend a shoe for him. And when he had mended it, he took out a ducat and gave it him.

When the poor shoemaker saw the ducat, he said, " Master, you have made me your debtor ; my work is a penny's worth, and you give me a ducat ! "

" My dear fellow," said the other, " if I choose to give it you, what need you care ? "

" May God requite you then," he answered, " it will help me and my children to live."

" So you have children ? " said the Jew.

" Ah, well, three girls, that's all."

" And how do you live ? "

" Well, as poor men must—from hand to mouth : a day's work for a day's meal."

" I am sorry for you, my man," says the other ; " but come with me, and I will give you a thousand ducats, if you will but leave your home. Only I must make a bargain with you, that when you see me open a paper and read, whatever you behold, you must not speak."

At hearing talk of a thousand ducats, the poor man, who,

when he saw a groat, thought it was a pound, answered him, "All right, I'll come."

So our friend, the Jew, paid him the ducats down, and he takes them, and brings them to his wife, and tells her how a man fell in with him, and gave him these ducats, but requires him to accompany him from home for a few days, and she is to take care of the house until his return.

Then he takes what he wants from the house, and goes and joins the Jew, and they start on their way.

They walked along, chaffing and laughing, until they came to a high mountain.

There the Jew takes out a piece of paper, and begins to read, whereupon our friend, the shoemaker, is silent ; and, all of a sudden, as the other reads, the mountain is cleft asunder and they enter in. They go down till they come to a castle, where the Jew gives a knock, and the door opens, and they behold a maiden inside, fair as a fresh fountain, who straightway addresses the Jew with the words, "Alas ! are you not yet weary of tormenting me ? " And with that she takes her kerchief off and gives it him. And as the Jew kept on reading, she took off one garment after another and gave it him.

Now the shoemaker looked on but said nothing, waiting what should happen ; but, at length, when he saw that the girl was left with nothing on but her shirt, he could contain himself no longer, but said to the Jew : " Come, I say, this is too bad, why you'll strip the girl ! " And that moment both Jew and maiden vanished from his eyes.

So when the cobbler was left alone, he walked about the castle, and beheld ducats and dollars and all sorts of coin, and said to himself, " Ah, if only it were possible to find my way out, I might take some home."

At length he enters a chamber, where he finds a chandelier of diamond. " Eh ! " he cries, " what a fine chandelier."

And he goes to take hold of it and finds that it will unscrew. Then he takes it and unscrews it and puts the pieces in his fob, and looks for a place where he can get out. After a long while he sees a part of the building where the light comes through a little hole. So the poor shoemaker ran eagerly forward, and as he drew nearer and nearer (it was his last hope, poor fellow !) he said, " Either I shall die here, or the lucky star of my children will help me out."

So he made his way into the shaft and, little by little, he came out at the foot of the mountain and said, " Glory be to God that I am safe out of that hell ! " And he ran home as fast as he could. When his wife saw him she said :

" Welcome back, husband ! how have you fared ? "

" Ill and chill ! good wife," he answered. " How I'm alive I know not, but either I had more years yet to live, or my daughters' good luck preserved me ! "

Then he takes out the chandelier and screws it together and hangs it up in the middle of his parlour. And in the evening, when they sat down to supper, he says, " Well, my dear wife, let us light up the chandelier, and make merry and rejoice. For I was as good as lost, but God is gracious."

And when they had lit the chandelier, forty maidens, fair as the fresh fountains, appear, loaded with treasure, and each one with a musical instrument in her hand, and say to him :

" Take this, our mistress sends it for the favour you have shown her ! "

And after supper, they begin to play, and to dance, that it was a sight to see ! That evening the vizier happened to be passing in the street below, and he heard the dancing and the music, and ran up-stairs to look ; and he sees the chandelier and forty damsels, each one playing on an instrument and dancing like mad.

The next day he runs straight to the King, for he was jealous of the shoemaker's joy, and says to him :

" Oh, King, I used to think that no one was so well off as you ; but last night I went to the house of a shoemaker, and there are such good things as you have not got."

" And what then did you see there ? "

" Why," said he, " there is a chandelier of diamond and forty maidens, fair as the fresh fountains, singing and dancing in a way which it's one thing to tell of and quite another thing to see ! "

" Vizier, is it the truth you are telling me ? "

" Indeed, your majesty, it is : and if it please you, come with me this evening and see for yourself."

K

Well, on hearing such a tale, the King dons his mufti when evening came, and goes with the vizier to the shoemaker's before the chandelier was lighted. And the King was astonished at its beauty. After a while the shoemaker proceeds to light it, and that moment the forty maidens appear, each one with a bag of money in her hand, and give it to him and say, "Take this with our lady's thanks for the favour you have shown her."

And then they begin to dance and sing, so that the King was beside himself with wonder, and sat and sat until the damsels had gone away : and then he goes to the palace and straightway sends word to the cobbler to send him the diamond chandelier. What could the poor man do ?

> "When kings proclaim the law
> No dog may stir a paw!"

So he takes it and brings it to the King. And straightway they seize the shoemaker and put him in prison. This then was the favour shown him! With his wealth he found misfortune!

In the evening, then, our friend the King and his vizier lighted up the chandelier, and eagerly awaited the arrival of the maidens, but instead of any maidens coming there came forty negroes with their cudgels and begin to belabour the King and the vizier with, "Here's for you!" and "There's for you!" till they felt the vengeance of heaven on their heads : and they tell them that they must without fail set free the shoemaker and give him his chandelier, or they would be the death of them : and then they went away. Next day the vizier proposed to the King, not to give up the chandelier, but only to get the shoemaker himself to light it for them that evening. Accordingly when night fell they fetch the shoemaker to the palace and tell him to light the chandelier. But no sooner did he light it, than, lo, and behold! there came forty negroes, angrier than ever, and began to belabour King and vizier again, till they were at their wits' end ; and cried, "You dogs! what did we tell you?"

"Let us alone!" answered the vizier and the King: "and to-morrow we will let him have it."

So the negroes went away again ; but when next day came they still did not give it up, but decided he must fetch his wife as well, that she may light it with her own hand. As they

decided so they did. They summon the woman, and tell her to
light it. But that evening things went worse than ever. No
sooner does she light it, than behold the forty negroes, ready to
kill them outright and crying, " Nay, but you are past all bearing !
The first day you tell us, 'We'll give it him !' and the next day
you tell us, 'We'll give it him !' It seems you have not yet
enough taste of the cudgel."

And they set to work at once on the vizier and the King, until
no one could have seen them without compassion. They
drubbed them to that degree that they were in bed for a month.
Then they take the chandelier out and bring it to the shoemaker's
house. And next night he lights it again, and the forty maidens
come. But when the vizier and the King were well of their
wounds, the vizier goes again one evening to the shoemaker's to
see if the maidens still visit him, and he comes and finds them
dancing. Then he runs to the King, and says to him, " This
will never do, that a shoemaker should have such enjoyment,
and your Majesty should be without it. But as he has daughters,
let your son take the eldest, and tell him he must give the
chandelier for her dowry."

" Well said, vizier," replies the King; and forthwith they send,
and call for the shoemaker, and tell him so.

" As your Majesty commands," answers the shoemaker, " not
only the chandelier but more besides."

So they decide that the wedding shall take place at once, and
they send and fetch the bride and the chandelier, and bring
them to the palace, and in the evening, when they proceed to
light the chandelier, the forty maidens come, and say to the
shoemaker, " Our lady bids us tell you not to marry your
daughter until she comes herself. Otherwise she will take away
both the chandelier, and all she has given you besides."

" Very good !" says the King. " Let us not marry her to
night, but wait till she comes herself."

And the next evening, when they lit the chandelier, they heard
from afar shouts and songs, and knew they were bringing their
lady. So she came into the palace, and they all gave her glad
welcome ; and then they kept the wedding, and there were
rejoicings and revels ; and then the maiden told her story ; how

that she was a King's daughter, and the Jew had wooed her, and she refused, and on that account the Jew had enchanted her, and buried her in the mountain; and that when her father learned that she was in the mountain, he went and dug there and built the castle; and the Jew used to go and torment her every hour, and tried to compass her destruction, for which end, she said, it was necessary that the Jew should have another man with him, and if he held his peace until the maiden was stripped, then she would be destroyed, and the third person as well: but if on the other hand he spoke then only the Jew would be destroyed: and this was why he took the shoemaker on the understanding that he was not to speak; but he did speak, and the Jew was delivered over to the vengeance of heaven. And she went on to say that she would take up her abode with the shoemaker's daughter. And he soon married his other two daughters and they lived right happily, and we here happier still.

THE TALE OF THE DRAGON.

(TENOS.)

———:o:———

ONCE on a time there was a man who, as he was walking along, found a pea, and said to himself, " I will plant this pea and when the pea-stalk grows up it will bear many peas, and so I shall be able one day to lade ships with them, perhaps even the twelve ships of the King. With that thought in his head he got up and went to find the King and have an audience with him. So he presented himself before him and asked him for his twelve ships, that he might lade them—with his one pea ! which he had in his shoe. When the King heard the words of this young hero, he said to him, " If it please you I have a daughter whom I think worthy of you." But I forgot to tell you that this man, as he was going to see the King, met with a dragon, who said to him, "Whither away ? " " To seek my fortune," he replied. " Your fortune is made if you prove able to answer me ten questions," answered the dragon, " but otherwise you are lost. And if on the other hand you do answer the ten questions, you will be presented with that palace that you see there, as it is, with all its belongings, gardens and estates, and I shall burst asunder as soon as you answer me all my questions."

Let us leave the dragon, then, who had made this bargain with Penteclemás (for so the young man was called), and let us come to speak of the King who desires him for a son-in-law.

Now poor Penteclemás thought if he were to say " No ! " the King would not believe his word and would not let him have the ships. So he thought he had better say " Yes ! " and see how things turned out. When he had given his consent, the King, in order to assure himself whether he was rich or poor, gave orders to a servant to put ragged sheets and a torn coverlid on his bed, for Penteclemás to pass the night on. And when night fell he said to him, " Go to your chamber, for it is time to sleep." The King told the servant to watch all night long to see whether he went to sleep or not, " For," said he, " if he sleep, it is a sign he is poor ; but if he do not sleep it shows he has been accustomed to new bed-clothes and cannot sleep on rags." In the morning the servant tells him that Penteclemás was restless all the night and never closed his eyes. Then the King orders him on the following night to lay the bed properly and with due regard to comfort. And not to make a long tale of it, in the good bed our young hero sleeps as sound as sound could be, because he had no fear of losing his pea in this bed. So the King was satisfied that he was a youth of good birth, and married him to his daughter.

But the reason why he had not slept the first night was not because of the ragged bed-clothes, but only because he was afraid of losing the pea and not being able to find it.

After a time he began to think of what he should say to the dragon, since the time was drawing near—forty days' grace having been fixed.

When the wedding had taken place about three days, our young hero wished to leave home, and the Princess desired to accompany him. Accordingly a considerable retinue followed in her train, and her husband, Penteclemás, went to the dragon's castle in order to learn his fate, and see what would befall him. He went on in front, and a short distance behind followed his wife with her train of attendants. Penteclemás said to them, " If the Princess asks whose are these estates, mind you tell her they belong to Penteclemás. This can do you no harm. " And as luck would have it the Princess actually did ask once or twice about the estates, and when she heard they belonged to her husband she was very much pleased. But the unfortunate Penteclemás kept thinking over the words of the dragon, and what sort of questions he would ask him ; for the time allowed was drawing to an end.

When they arrived at the dragon's castle, he and his wife went up the steps, and the rest of the company took their leave. Penteclemás was very thoughtful. His wife said to him, " What ails you ? " " Nothing," said he, for what should he answer her, and how was he to tell her what was going to happen, when the time for the dragon's approach drew near ? At last an old woman from the neighbourhood saw the wife of Penteclemás sorrowful.

" What ails you ? " she asked. She answered, " Seeing my husband sad and thoughtful, I am sad as well."

Then the old woman goes to Penteclemás and puts the same question to him. What had he to hope from the old woman ? So he hid his thoughts from her, till at last she got impatient, and then he told her. The old woman consoled him, saying, that when the dragon came she would answer the questions he put, and that he was never to mind the dragon at all, but only to comfort the Princess who was so sorrowful.

When the dragon came he called out, " Are you there ? " "Glad to see you ! " shouts the old woman, pretending to be Penteclemás . Then they close the doors and the dragon and the old woman are shut up together in the castle.

The dragon cries, " What does one stand for ? "

" One stands for God ! " cries the old woman

Dragon : " What does two stand for ? "

Old Woman : " Even-handed justice ! "

Dragon : " What does three stand for ? "

Old Woman : " The three legs of the trivet that they put the pot on."

Dragon : " What does four stand for ? "

Old Woman : " The four teats of the cow."

Dragon : " What does five stand for ? "

Old Woman : " The five fingers of our hands."

Dragon : " What does six stand for ? "

Old Woman : " The six stars in the constellation Pleiades."

Dragon : " What does seven stand for ? "

Old Woman : " A dance of seven damsels."

Dragon : " What does eight stand for ? "

Old Woman : "The eight tentacles of the eight-footed octopus."

Dragon : " What does nine stand for ? "

Old Woman : " Nine months your mother bare you."

Dragon : " What does ten stand for ? "

Old Woman : " Why that's your own number. Burst, dragon, burst ! "

So the dragon burst, and Penteclemás inherited the castle and all its belongings, and lived happily with the Princess, and they loaded the old woman with money.

LITTLE JOHN, THE WIDOW'S SON.

(UPPER SYRA.)

———— :o: ————

ONCE on a time there was a King who had a hunter in his employ. He gave him his rations, his butter, and his oil, but all the game he killed he had to bring to the King. One day, when he was going to bring his game to the King, he had to pass by the vizier's. The vizer wanted to get them from him, but he at once refused, in accordance with the charge entrusted to him. The vizier was very angry with him, and sought to compass his destruction in every possible way. But the huntsman was very shrewd, and he could find no occasion against him.

At length the time came when he grew old, and his end was approaching. Then he called his wife to him and said, " Wife, I am dying. Do you look after my boy and continue to keep him at school, and if he asks you at any time what was his father's trade, mind you do not tell him. For out of spite against me the vizier might find some occasion to destroy him." And when he had said these words to her he died.

Now the lad, as long as his father was alive, used to go properly dressed to the school. But after his death, on the King stopping the salary, he would go shoeless and ragged.

So he used to hear the neighbours say, " If that boy's father were alive, do you think he would go badly dressed ? "

Next day, therefore, he asked his mother what trade his father was. But she, remembering her father's charge, told him, in order to put him off, that his father was a tailor. When he went again to school he heard the same things said ; and then he asked of his mother what trade his father had followed.

She devised a thousand tricks to satisfy him, but when she could not do so, at length she said, " Your father's profession was the chase, and the King found us food and pay, and we were well off."

The boy went all that week to school, and on Sunday said to his mother that she should give him his father's bow and arrows, that he might go out for a walk. So he went away early in the morning and set off to hunt. It was his luck to kill a number of birds. He took them and brought them along to the King. He then continued to go daily. Hunting suited him, and he killed a quantity of game, and always brought it straight to the King.

Then the King asks, " What man is this that brings the game ? "

They tell him it is Little John, the widow's boy, the son of his former huntsman.

Then the King called him and said, " Are you the son of the huntsman I used to have ? "

He said, " I am."

Says the King, " I will take you in your father's place."

And for every five pounds weight his father had brought him he caught him twice as much.

So the lad used to come and go daily. But one day, as he passed by the vizier's, to go to the King, the vizier saw him, and the birds took his fancy, and he asked them of him. But the lad, whose charge was even stricter than his father had received, would not give them him but brought them to the King. The vizier therefore conceived a great spite against him, and strove by every means in his power to find occasion against him to destroy him.

One day the King sends word to him as follows : " This week you must go into the country and remain out, not returning to town until the Saturday ; and all the game you kill you must keep and bring to me, for on the Sunday I shall give a banquet to my ministers."

So the boy went away on the Monday and sought the open country. The whole of that day he ranged the fields up and down and could find nothing. To be short, he kept searching for game until the Saturday, and not only could he not find a bird, but not even so much as a feather.

On the Saturday, then, when it was now about noon, he despaired, and said, " Oh God, what misfortune is mine ! and with what face shall I approach the King? Better that some wild beast should come and eat me than that I should go empty-handed to the King."

While he was thus speaking, on a sudden there appeared a wild beast, like none other in the world. Its skin was all covered with priceless jewels. When the lad saw it, he was seized with great terror, and began to ply his arrows. For more than two hours he fought with the beast, until he slew it; and when at last he had killed it he went close to it, and the skin of the monster gleamed with the diamonds and precious stones which it had on it. He takes it and skins it, and carries away the hide. And as he had no birds, he makes off to the town with it and brings it to the King. As he passed by the vizier's he at once demanded it of him. But the lad refused to give it to him, though he offered him fifty thousand piastres for it. But the lad was indignant, and went off and brought it to the King. When the King beheld it—such a sight as was never seen in the world before—he ordered the vizier to pay him ten thousand piastres reward. But the vizier only gave him one hundred.

The King then called his court together to show it to them. On seeing it every one said that no kingdom under heaven had such a thing to show.

But the vizier only said, "That hide is very handsome; but if you had the bones of elephants to build a church with, all the kings of the earth would come to admire it, and to see the hide as well."

Says the King, "But how can we kill the elephants, when we need a hundred thousand soldiers to keep watch against them lest they come and devour us men?"

The vizier answers, "Little John here was able to kill a monster like that, and he will be able to bring us the elephants' bones."

Then the King calls him and tells him the matter.

Little John replies, "I will go home, and in a while I will give you my answer."

So Little John goes home sorrowful. His mother observes him and says, "Come, let us eat."

Says he, "I have no appetite."

Says she, "What is the matter with you?"

He was unwilling to tell her, but she urged him so much, that he sits down and relates it all to her.

She said, " Never fear, sit down to your supper and I will tell what I have heard from your sire."

They sat down and ate, and when the meal was finished, his mother says to him :

" Tell the King that he must give you a thousand men with axes, and another thousand with buckets, and a thousand horses loaded with wine, and another thousand loaded with gunpowder; the expenses to be borne by the vizier." This he tells to the King, and the King ordered the vizier, in three days' time, to have the things ready at his own cost. The vizier said to himself, " Let him go, if it's only that he may perish, and I will pay for it."

Then Little John went away to his mother, and asked her how he was to slay the elephants. Says she, " My son, in the place where you are going there are a hundred elephants, and every midday, when they are thirsty, they come down into the plain where the lake is, and drink water. You must go by night and set the thousand men with buckets to empty the lake, and pour in the wine and the gunpowder, stir it up well, and then bide your time, and at midday they will come, thirsty with the heat, and will rush into the lake to drink ; they will get drunk and dizzy, and then fall asleep ; and then the men must be ready with their axes to go in among them, and hew them to pieces, and take their bones, and load their horses with them, that you may bring them to the King."

Little John did as she told him, and when the King saw the bones, he ordered the vizier to pay him fifteen thousand piastres. But the vizier only paid him fifty. Then the King began to build the church, and when he had finished it, he called the ministers, the vizier and the courtiers to see it. Well, there was a church such as was not to be found in any other kingdom. But the vizier said to him :

" As for the church, men will come from all parts to see it ; but let me tell you in such and such a place there is a dragon's daughter, who has forty brothers that guard her, for besides her beauty, she has the virtue that whoever shall kiss her becomes of the age of twenty-two, and many kings have wished to get her ;

Russia alone has lost over five hundred thousand soldiers on her account."

Says the King, " How is it possible that we should win her, when Russia was unable to do so ? "

" I wonder, your majesty, to hear you speak thus when you see Little John, the widow's son, who went and got the elephants' bones. Surely he is able to fetch the dragon's daughter, too."

The King, who was very old, and remembered the pleasure he had in his youth, straightway summons Little John, and commands him to go and fetch her.

Little John went away to his mother full of sadness. His mother said to him :

" Why, my lad, what ails you ? won't you tell me ? "

" What shall I tell you, mother dear ? The King desires so-and-so."

"Never mind," says she, I will instruct you what to do, for you must know, these are tricks of the vizier. But go and tell the King as follows : ' By force, we shall never get her, but let your majesty give me a good steed, and I will go and try my best to fetch her.' "

The King gave him leave to go into the stable, and choose whichever pleased him best. Accordingly, he goes and equips himself, and his mother says to him :

" My son, it is no use your coming back here again, for the vizier will spoil everything for you, but take all the money we have and go and settle in another country."

The lad kissed his mother's hand, received her blessing, and departed. Then he walked along the high road five or six days' journey. As he went, he came to a river which was very broad, so that he could not cross it. There was a negro stooping down with one of his lips on one side of the river, and the other at the other—a very devil of a mouth. He touches him with his foot and says to him, " What are you doing here ? "

" Oh, I sit here till somebody comes by, and then I suck the river dry, and let him cross."

" Well, then, suck away," says he.

In a moment he sucked it up, and Little John crossed to the other side, and said to the negro :

" Well done, my brave, to suck up such a river as that ! " ·

The negro answers him, " No brave am I, only Little John, the widow's son deserves that name."

Says he, " I am Little John, the widow's son."

Says the other, " Welcome, master, have you any need of my company ? "

When Little John saw what a man he was, he said, " Come along."

So the two got up, and went on their way together.   As they were going along, they saw a man who was carrying two hills in his hands, and playing with them.   They weren't so very large : one was about the size of Pyrgos, and the other of Kappare [the two highest mountains in Syra].   He says to him, " Holloa, what are you doing there ? "

He answered, " My fingers are numb, and I want to unstiffen them."

Said the other, " Well done, my brave fellow, to carry mountains like that in order to relieve your fingers ! "

He replied in the same terms as the negro had, and Little John took him along with him, and they went further.   Some way on they met another man, who had uprooted some hundred trees or so, and was binding them in bundles.

Said Little John, " What are you doing there ? "

He replied, " I am making a little load of wood to carry to my mother, for her to cook the dinner with."

Says he, " Well done, my brave fellow, to make a mountain of wood serve as a single load."

He replies like the rest, and now there were four of them.

As they went on, they met another, a little man, who kept running hither and thither, and they no sooner saw him than they lost him from view, and then caught sight of him again, coming towards them.   When he came to a standstill, Little John asked " What are you doing ? "

" Oh," he answered, " one moment I'm in Stamboul, the next in Europe ; wherever I want, I go in a trice."

Says he, " Well done, my brave fellow."

" No brave am I," replies the other, " that is the name of Little John, the widow's son."

" Why, I am Little John, the widow's son," says he.

" Welcome, master," was the answer. " Do you want me to come with you ? "

" Come along ! " said he. So they all went on together, till they meet with one who was lying on the ground, with his ear against the earth. Little John asks him, " Pray, what are you doing there ? "

He motions him to be quiet.

Then he pushes him with his foot, and says, " What are you after ? "

" I'm listening," he answers, " to hear what is taking place in the under-world."

The same conversation then took place as before, and he tells him to come along with them. They then journeyed on for a month—two months—three months, and saw nothing but sky and earth. At length, one day, they see something white, like a pigeon. So they went on, and the nearer they came, the larger it got. When they came up to it, they saw a castle, and, outside it, a fountain ; and they sat down. In a little while, the earth and the hills began to rumble, and they see forty dragons coming towards them. When the dragons saw the men, they said, " Here's luck for us. What do you want here ? "

Says Little John, "We have come to fetch the dragon's daughter."

They answer, " If you are able to win three wagers which we shall lay you, then you may take the dragon's daughter ; but, if not, and you but lose one, then we shall eat you up."

" What is the first ? "

The dragons had a cauldron about half as large as our Market-place, and it had forty handles round it : and in it they were boiling forty oxen. So the dragons said, " If you are able to take that cauldron down from the trivet, and eat the food that it contains, you will win the first wager."

Then says Little John, " You that sucked up the river, are you able to eat all that food ? "

Says he, " Of course I am ! "

So our friend the negro takes a step forward and puts one finger into one ring, and another into the opposite one—for his palms were not large enough to grasp the cauldron—raises it up aloft, and holds it in mid-air, and says to Little John :

"Am I to swallow cauldron and all, or only the meat ? "

"Only the meat."

Then he opens his lips, and turns up the cauldron to his mouth, and empties it completely out.

Then said the eldest dragon, "Well ! you've won the first wager."

Says little John, " What is the next ? "

The tower had a brazen gate, and unless the whole forty dragons went in at it, they could not open it.

" To open the gate, is the second wager," said the dragons.

Then said Little John, " Ho ! you who were carrying mountains to unstiffen your fingers, are you able to open that gate ? "

" Yes, master." But he rather thought he might not open it, so he took a run at it. He gave it a push, and in it goes, hinges and all !

Then Little John asks once more, "What's the last wager ? "

Now the dragon's daughter had two accomplishments. She could turn into a dove and fly in the air ; and she could also become a garden of flowers, and lemon trees, and all sweet-smelling shrubs. Accordingly the dragons tell them :

" In such and such a place there is a spring. You must take each a cup, and the one who gets there first has won the wager."

" But," says Little John, " who will be there to see ? "

They answer, "Whoever gets there first, the water that he fetches will be clear ; afterwards it will be troubled, and turn muddy."

Then says Little John to the one who could be wherever he chose in a trice, " Are you equal to this task ? "

" Of course I am," says he.

So they place the cup in his hands, and at once the dragon's daughter turns into a dove, and she and the dwarf start off, and are soon out of sight. When they had vanished, Little John ordered him who put his ear to the ground in order to listen what they were saying in the under world—to find out who was in front. So he put down his ear to the ground, and said :

" The dragon's daughter has turned into a garden, and the

dwarf has gone to sleep. Now the dragon's daughter is off again!"

Then Little John shouted, "Ho! you who were uprooting the cypress trees, blow a blast to make a noise, and see whether he won't wake up." With that he tore up the cypress trees, and the dwarf woke up, and set off running, and passed the dragon's daughter, and reached the spring and filled his cup, before the dragon's daughter and returns; so that the three wagers were won!

Then they took the dragon's daughter and went off with her. When they had gone an hour's journey, the dragons say:

"Is it not a disgrace to us, forty brothers as we are, that seven fellows should carry off our sister?"

"Let's go and fetch her back!" So they started in pursuit to devour them, and regain the dragon's daughter. Little John hearing the uproar, turned round and saw the dragons running after them. At his bidding, the one who tore up trees to make bundles of them, blew down a few cypress trees, and they continued their march. When they came to the place where he had been crouching who held his ear to the ground, he desired to remain behind; they leave him, and so on; as they came to the place where each had joined them they dismissed him, until only Little John and the dragon's daughter were left. He begins to tell her the story of his life. When he had done, the dragon's daughter says to him, "Never fear! I will frustrate the designs of your friend, the vizier."

When they arrived at the city, the King sent his musicians to escort the dragon's daughter into town, and they brought her before the King. Then she said to him:

"I am yours; but I wish you to make a banquet, and to invite your council, the vizier, the ministers and courtiers, for I have a speech to make to them."

So the King summoned them all, and the dragon's daughter spoke as follows:

"Suppose a man had a trusty servant, and when he orders his clerk to give him a hundred piastres, he only gave him ten, what would the clerk deserve?"

Then they all declared and subscribed the sentence, that he

should be tied to four horses, and the horses should be set running and tear him in pieces. Then the dragon's daughter said further, "This is the punishment due to the vizier, for thus and thus has he behaved to Little John." So they fasten the precious vizier to four horses, whip the horses, and he is rent into four quarters.

Then the King kissed the dragon's daughter, and made our friend Little John his vizier; and then they kept

> "Wedding feast with dance and song,
> And carousals loud and long."

THE SCAB-PATE.

(ASTYPALÆA.)

———:o:———

Once on a time there was a King and a Queen, and they had three sons and one daughter.

One evening the King says to his sons :

" My lads, this evening when you go to sleep, whatever dream each of you have, you must come to-morrow morning and tell it me."

" Good, father," the boys answer, and each goes to his bed. They fall asleep, and all three dream. Early in the morning the King awakes, and waits to hear the dreams of his sons, for by that means he desired to find out the fate of each.

First of all then, the eldest son comes and says to him, " Good morning, father."

" The same to you, my son," he answers.

"Well, how did you pass the night? Did you have a dream?"

" I did indeed, father," he answered.

" Well, and what was it ike ? "

"I thought," said he, " that I held in my hands cities, lands, manservants and maidservants, and the like."

" Well done, my son," he answers, and at once divided to him his portion.

He goes away and the second comes. He too wishes his father good day. " The same to you, my son," replies his father.

And what do you think ? He too had seen the same dream as his brother, and the same hour he divided to him his portion.

Let us now come to the youngest of all. He had dreamt that his father was carrying a pitcher and a towel, and poured him out water to wash with. Now the lad, who had his wits about him, considered with himself and said, " Well, seeing my father pouring out water for me to wash with is as much as saying that I shall be better than my father, and if he hears that perhaps he will slay me ; and again, if I say that I had no dream at all, he will regard me as born to bad luck, and it will be worse for me." So he did not know what to do. He thought and thought, and after a long time he said to himself, "I'll say I saw nothing, let come what will !" And he arose and came to his father.

"Good morning, father," says he.

"The same to you, my son. Did you dream aught last night ? "

"Nothing, father."

"Fie, for shame ! "

"Well, what can I tell you when I saw nothing ? "

Then the King's countenance was changed, and he said to himself, "Ah ! that bodes no good ; he is an illstarred youth and I may come to bad luck some day on his account. But it is better to get rid of him, for an unlucky man may do what he likes, he will never get on."

And forthwith he calls his executioner and tells him to take the lad into the pleasure-grounds for a walk (and this he said that the lad might not suspect anything, but he reckoned without his host). And afterwards he said in secret to the executioner, that he should take him into a desert place and kill him, and bring him as a token his shirt and his little finger.

Now the lad understood all this, but what could he do ?

So the executioner takes him and instead of leading him into the pleasure grounds for a walk he takes him into the woods.

But you see the executioner had not the heart to kill such an angel of a youth, whom his father was sending to an unmerited death ; and his distress was so great that his eyes ran rivers of tears. When the Prince saw that, he said, "What ails you that you weep, my friend ? "

The other, unable to divulge so sad a secret, replied, " I remembered past misfortune, and it made me weep." Then he answered him, " Listen, my friend. Let me tell you I know very well that my father told you to kill me, and wherefore should you hide it from me ? If you don't tell me now, you will have to tell me some time. My father had no pity on me, and yet you pity me ? "

"Ah, Prince," he answers, " I cannot do such a thing, let

your father do with me what he likes. But the worst of it is that he required tokens at my hands, namely, your bloodstained shirt and your little finger."

"Slay me not," answered the other, "and as for the tokens that is an easy matter, and I will swear by heaven and earth to you that I will not come down into the town." And he at once stripped off his shirt and gave it to the executioner, then he turned his face away and said to him, "Come, my friend, cut off my finger!" So he cuts his finger off and they dip the shirt in the blood, and then the Prince says to him, "Take these things and bring them to my father, and leave me that the wild beasts may devour me, or I perish with hunger."

So they take leave of one another and each one goes his way, the executioner to the King and the young man to the forest. When the King saw the tokens he supposed without doubt that the executioner had slain his son, and he had no further concern. But God has vengeance even for the slain! As for him he was scouring the hills and dales and living only on herbs, so that. he became weak and wan, and his garments were tattered, and he went he knew not whither. In six months' time he espied one day a castle. Then said he to himself, "I may as well perish one way as another, for as it is, either I shall die of hunger or the beasts will eat me." So he arose and came to the castle. He entered it, and looked this way and that, but neither man nor anything else met his eye; except only one or two pails and pots. Says he, "Well, I'll stop here and see what happens. To suppose that nobody lives here—dragons if not men—is out of the question." So he remained where he was, and close upon mid-day he beholds a dragon, driving from pasture a thousand sheep, which he was bringing towards the castle. At the sight of such a monster the Prince's blood congealed in his veins, but whither should he flee for safety? Moreover, as the monster came nearer to the castle the Prince's heart regained a little of its courage, for he saw that the dragon was stone blind. Accordingly he crept away into a corner, and the dragon comes and takes a pail and begins to milk the sheep. Then the lad comes along stealthily with a bottle and takes a little milk and drinks it, for he was faint and famished. Afterwards he sees our friend the dragon, who had finished milking, take the pail and quaff the milk at a draught, and wipe his moustache and beard, and take a pipe with a bowl, into which—heaven save us !—he put about seven pounds of tobacco; he sat down in his chair to smoke. Then thought the lad, now is the time to play him a trick. So he crept up to him, and said, " Father, behold your son, if you are pleased to adopt me."

"Who is that talking to me," says the dragon. "But come, I will soon see if you are my son. I will give you three blows with my fist, and if you can stand them, I will call you my son. If not, go about your business."

" All right," he answers, and quick as quick could be, he gets three sacks, and fills them full of chaff and goes close to the dragon, and calls out, " Strike away, father." The dragon, who could not see, lifted his fist and struck the sack and burst it into fragments, and says to him, " Well, are you alive ? "

" I'm alive, father !" he answers. " Very good," he replied, " you shall have two more."

And to make a short story of it, with his cunning he persuaded the dragon to adopt him as his son, and he loved him like his life.

Then he said to him, " My son, you see how I fare upon milk, but do you take this diamond wand, and when you are hungry, wave it to one side, and there will appear before you a table covered with all kinds of dishes and sweets, and all manner of dainties, and when you have eaten your fill wave it in the other direction, and it will vanish away from you. And you shall live in the castle and eat and drink as you list, and lend me a helping hand with the sheep, for alas ! I am blind."

" Good father," he answers, "whatsoever you bid me, I will do."

Then the dragon takes the sheep and leads them out to pasture. At once the lad takes the wand in order to see if the dragon's words are true. So he waves it one way, and forthwith there appears a table spread with dishes, wines, sweets, and everything required for a meal. So our friend the Prince sits down, for mind you he was so hungry he could hardly see, and he tucked in fit to burst. Then when he had eaten his fill he waved the wand the other way, and the table vanished from before him. Then said he, " Eh, well is me ! now I have made my fortune."

Then he goes and tidies up the castle, and puts everything into its place, lights a fire, washes up the pails; and when the dragon comes and finds everything arranged to his liking, he was delighted beyond measure.

So the two spent a pleasant life together, and the dragon now began to thank God for sending him a son to look after him in his old age.

One day, as the Prince was minding the castle, he finds a little flute in a little niche, and he began to play it, when everything began to dance: the castle danced; he looked out of the window, the hills, the fields, the trees, all were dancing, so that it was a treat for any one to see them.

Then the Prince puts it in his bosom, and the next day in the morning, he says to the dragon :

" Father, I should like to go and feed our sheep to-day, in order to relieve you, as you are blind."

" Nay, my son," said he, "you are not used to such matters; do you but stay in the house, for I don't get tired."

Then the Prince said to him, "May you have no luck with me, father, if you don't let me go just for once this day to enjoy myself; and if you don't wish, I'll never go another time."

Then the dragon, not wishing to vex him, said to him :

" My lad, as you are so eager to do so, take our sheep ; but be very careful not to go to that high hill, for up there there dwell some water-fairies, and when any one comes into their quarters, either they take his sight away, or do him some other mischief. It is now thirty-two years since I have been blinded for going there, and may you never know what I suffer ! "

" Good ! my father," he replies; " do you think me mad that I should rush into the fire of my own accord, and burn myself ! "

So he takes the sheep and drives straight away to that very hill, where the dragon had told him not to go. That was a region whither no bird ever winged its way, but it was one mass of grass, and the good sheep at the sight of it, buried their faces in it, and ate and ate until they were tired, so that their udders were filled with milk, and could contain it no longer, while he went into a tree and played upon the flute.

At the top of the mountain the water-fairies had their castle, and one of them looked out of the window and espies the sheep and the Prince up in the tree, and then she says to her companion:

"Eh! here's a fine treat for us to-day, sister, look out and see!"

And both of them rush out and try to catch him. He, as we said, was up in the tree, playing his flute. So they come up to the foot of it, and tell him to come down. But he pipes away at his tune. Well! they try to catch him, but in vain, for one moment they are low down, and the next they are high up, and at length, just as one of them is going to grasp him, he makes a dart and seizes her by the hair and twists them round a branch, and hangs her up like a bunch of grapes. Then the other goes to the rescue of her sister, and meets with the same fate. Then he says to them:

"I have you nicely, wretches!"

They entreat him to let them down, and they promise whatever he desires.

Then he says, "If you will restore my father's sight, the dragon, I will let you down, but not otherwise."

"By all means," said they, "only let us down, for we have got it up there in the castle."

"No," said he, "tell me where you keep it, that I may go and fetch it myself, and then I will set you free."

Then they point to the castle, and tell him he must go and find two young water-fairies sitting by a fire and cooking, and he must take care when he goes in not to say "Bo!" or he will frighten them away, but say "Chuck, chuck," and caress them, and then ask them for his father's eyes, which are on the shelf in a box, in the shape of two golden apples; "and then," they continued, "come and take us down."

So the Prince sets off and reaches the castle. Now, on his way, he thought to himself:

"Ah, but there's some trick here. For when they tell me not to say 'Bo!' but only 'Chuck! chuck!' to their daughters, I'll be bound there's some dastardly plot at the bottom of it—by your leave—so I shall *not* do as they tell me."

According on his arrival, he looks in and shouts "Bo!" at the top of his voice, and forthwith our friends, the water-fairies' daughters, as they sat at the fire and warmed themselves, fell in and were burnt. Such it seems was their fate, and by this means, too, the Prince was saved, as otherwise they would have eaten him. Then he takes the box with the two golden apples in it, and departs.

The water-fairies all this time supposed he would do as they had bidden him, and that then their children would eat him; when there! all of a sudden, they espy him before them, and they say to one another, "Alack! the wretch has burned our children!" But what could they do? They put a good face on the matter, and said with a laugh—which was inwardly all venom—"Have you got your father's eyes?"

"I should rather think I had," he answers.

"Well, then, now let us down!"

"Good," says he, "wait first until I send my father, and he shall fetch you down!"

So he takes his sheep and goes off to the castle.

"Well! my lad, how did you fare," said the dragon.

"Right well, father."

Then the dragon milks half his flock, but he gets as much milk as at other times he was wont to get from the whole lot. The dragon was amazed, and said :

"Why, there's a good deal of milk to-day, my lad. All the time I've kept them I never got such a quantity."

"Well, you see, father, I have my eyes," replied the youth, "and I take them where I see plenty of grass, and that's the reason they yield plenty of milk."

When he had milked the rest of the sheep, and quaffed the milk, he sat down to smoke his pipe, and then the Prince said to him :

"Father, would you like this apple?"

And he gives him the golden apple.

"My son," says the dragon, "it's a strange thing where you could have found that apple, for there's abundance of everything else hereabouts, but I'm sure there are no apple-trees."

"Oh, father," he answers, "all these years that you have been bereft of your eyes, the hills have been covered with apple-trees. Do eat the apple."

"Nay! eat it yourself, my son, I don't care for apples."

"But I've eaten already," he answers, "as many as you can imagine."

So then the dragon eats the apple, and lo ! back comes one of his eyes !

When the poor dragon found he had regained his sight and could see the world, it seemed to him as though he had been dead and come to life again, and he falls on the youth's neck and embraces him, and covers him with kisses. "Oh, my son," he cries, "you have saved my life ! " And with that he takes out thirty-nine keys and gives them to him, and says, " My son, you are steward of all my possessions, and all that I have is yours, and I will serve you now as long as I live, and I will get you the fairest woman in the world for your wife, on account of the kindness which you have done me."

Then he gave him the other apple, and the dragon now had his sight completely restored. Then he asked him, " How has this good fortune befallen me, my son ? "

So the Prince proceeds to recount word by word what we need not repeat—and ends by telling him how he had hung up the water fairies and he might go and do what he liked with them. At the sound of such good news the dragon's heart was glad, and he exclaimed,

" Ah, at length the hour has come for me to work my will on them ! "

And he takes his sheep and goes straight to the place, and finds them hanging, as he desired, and rends them to pieces. When the dragon was gone the Prince took the keys and opened thirty-nine chambers ; and was half beside himself with wonder at the things he saw—money here ! diamonds and brilliants there ! In another room, gardens with golden trees and golden leaves, with a bird to every leaf ; then, fountains with golden fish swimming about, so that you would think it was a second Paradise : and his spirit was actually awe-struck at the marvels he beheld. Last of all he came to a door covered with black cobwebs, and tries first one key, and then another : not to detain you he tried the whole nine-and-thirty, but none of them would open it ; and at once he was out of humour because the dragon had not given him the key of that chamber.

When the dragon returned he saw he was vexed. "What ails you, my son, that you grieve?"—But he knew well enough!— "I hoped on my return to find you happy, after seeing so many sights, and I find you out of humour?"

"Ah, father," he said, "I took it for as certain as my life that you would give me all the keys; and there's just one chamber, where the cobwebs are, that you were afraid to give me the key of."

"My lad," he answers, "to allay your suspicions let me tell you there's nothing inside but coals and chaff. Therefore what would you gain by opening it? What do you expect to see there?"

The youth entreats him to give him the key, but the dragon refuses: and what with his extreme vexation he falls ill.

The poor dragon found himself in an evil plight, for on the one hand he loved the lad, and was fain to give him the key, but on the other he was sore afraid lest he might soon lose him, if he did; for you must know he had there locked up a mare, the like of which was not to be found in the whole world: in the twinkling of an eye it would vanish from view, for it could run like lightning; and, besides that, the worst of it was, it was very treacherous, and the dragon was afraid lest it might lead the lad astray with its words—for it could speak and all—and might take him and run off with him. But from the time when he had gone blind he had shut it up, and never opened the stable since. That was the reason why he did not wish to give the lad the key; but now that he saw how the youth was in danger of his life, he made up his mind to give it him. He also told him the reason of his unwillingness.

Then the Prince said to him, "Why, father, you treat me as if I had no sense at all, and was likely to get up and go away leaving so much enjoyment and such a mass of wealth behind me!" So the dragon gives him the key, and as the former goes away with his flock, our friend the Prince runs at once, all eagerness, to open the cobweb-covered door: and no sooner had he opened it than he beholds a mare, which was worth any sum you could name. But the poor beast was by this time in a sad plight, from being shut up so long in that place, without any one looking after it. The Prince, who was used to horses, was like to leap with joy; and at once takes it out, washes it, grooms it and gives it to eat, and henceforth that mare was the very life and soul of him. In the same chamber he found a little sword hung up, with these words written on the sheath, " Whosoever grasps this sword slays a thousand, and whosoever unsheathes it ten thousand." Accordingly he took the little sword also, and girds it on him. In the evening the dragon came, and at once sees that the lad is happy, for he smiled and said, " Now, father, you have granted the desire of my heart."

But he knew the serpent that was to devour him, and on that account was always sorrowful. Not to make too long a tale of it, for ten days or so, when the dragon was about to leave, the lad would rush off to the chamber and stroke the mare, and she in turn licked his hand, and played with him; and so he passed his time with the mare. When the ten days were over, while he was stroking her, she said, " Prince do you know that your father is in great danger; come let us go to his rescue ! "

The Prince looked this way and that, and when he heard that the mare could speak, he was beside himself with astonishment, and said, " What, my mare, can you talk? "

" Yes," she answered; " and I tell you your father is in danger, for he wanted to give his sister in marriage, and he has laid a wager which he who wins, is to marry her."

" And what may this wager be? " asks the Prince.

" He has made a lake and said, ' Whoever can cross this lake shall take the Princess to wife.' And princes and dukes keep coming and all perish ; and the end of it will be that the kings who lose their children will wage war on him, and he will finish by losing his life. But, if you are willing, we will go."

Now all children feel for their parents, and so the Prince, when he heard these words, forgot all the sufferings his father had caused him, and said to the mare, " Quick ! let us run to his rescue ! "

Then the mare tells him to take with him three saddles for her, and three suits for himself, one was to be the sky and the stars : the other the sea and the fishes, and the third the country with its flowers ; also he was to take a hair-comb, a cake of soap, and piece of salt and keep them all in readiness. She added moreover, " I have been for thirty-two years shut up, and have got quite stiff, and cannot run well at all. But you must fill three mattresses with chaff that I may jump about a little to get over my stiffness : and mind you have everything ready that I spoke of, for it may happen that while I am jumping, my shoe may strike against the ground and the dragon will hear it at once. You he will not harm, for he loves you ; but me he will tear in pieces."

So the Prince takes and fetches all that the mare had bidden him, and then stuffs the mattresses for the mare to jump on. While she was leaping for the third time, her shoe struck against the ground, and at once the dragon heard it and cried, " Ah, my son is leaving me."

So he deserts his sheep and runs in order to overtake them. But the mare, who knew it all, as soon as her shoe hit against the ground, said to the Prince, "Come! Have you got what I told you ? Quick ! jump up ! "

And the Prince jumps on her back, and they fly as fast as they can.

The dragon bursts into the castle. Neither mare nor boy were to be seen. Then he runs at once and opens a chamber, takes out a three-footed steed, mounts it and gives them chase. This three-footed mare was the sister of the one with four feet : and could run swifter than she, but she could not leap like the four-footed one. So as they rode, the mare told the Prince to be careful to look back from time to time, to see whether they were following them. He turned back accordingly on one occasion, and saw a black cloud, and told the mare. " Quick ! " she cries, " throw down the comb, for they have caught us up."

Then he throws it behind him, and it becomes a forest full of trees and shrubs, and the three-footed mare could not run a bit. And then they got a little ahead of them. But the poor three-footed mare had the forest on this side and that. She passed through it, and was after them again.

When she saw them near them again, the mare cried out that he should throw down the soap. So the Prince threw it, and it became a slippery cliff, so that when the three-legged mare attempted to run up she slipped and fell to the bottom; but after a long time she crossed the cliff also and came up with them again. And just as she was about to catch them the four-legged mare called to him to throw down the salt. The Prince, who was by this time rather dazed, and did not well know what he was about, throws the salt, indeed, but instead of throwing it behind he threw it in front, and straightway it became a lake as large as the sea.

Then the mare said to him, " Mercy on us, what have you done ? But never mind, only stick tight to my back."

And she takes a leap and just managed to clear it, for her hind legs touched the edge of the lake. And now the mare and the Prince sat down to rest, and, exhausted by their great efforts, stretched themselves on the ground as if they were dead.

The three-legged mare, with the dragon on her back, reaches the shore of the lake and then comes to a standstill. For, as we have said, she was a good runner, but she could not jump.

Then the dragon weeps and laments, crying, " Alack, my son! Have you no care for me ? Have you no care for the wealth and happiness you have left behind you? But, ah ! it is not your fault, but that of the accursed mare ! I was looking for this to happen some day. Go, my son, long life to you ; I trust you will yet remember me, and come some day to see me. For I shall never forget you ! " And much more in the same strain. Then he arises and returns to his castle.

Afterwards our friend the mare gets up with the Prince as soon as they were well rested, and they recommence their journey.

As they were going along they came to a fountain with two spouts, the one ran gold and the other silver. And the mare told the Prince to take and dip her mane, part of it in the gold, and part in the silver, and lastly the whole of her body ; and also to take and dip his finger into the silver. The Prince did as the mare bade him, and his finger became silvered over; and as for the mare, she was a sight too dazzling to behold, all golden in one place and all silver in another.

Afterwards he says to him, " Further on our way we shall meet a man leading a lame horse to the market to sell. Now you are to give him whatever he asks for it, so that you secure that horse for we have need of it. And you must give him your dress, and make him give you his."

Accordingly on the road the met a peasant who was leading a lame horse, as the mare had foretold. And the Prince said to him, " Where is it you are going to, my good man ? "

" Where am I going ? " said he. " Alack ! alack ! this horse of mine, here, was all my livelihood. And it fell down and broke its leg, and I am now going to the town to sell it."

" Sell it to me," said the Prince.

At hearing this the poor man thought it very strange that a man who had such a mare as was not to be equalled all the world over should ask him to sell him his lame horse.

" Ah, sir," said he, " you want to make fun of me. What good can this lame horse of mine do you ? But you fine gentlemen are always ready to have your laugh at us poor men."

But the Prince answered him, " I am quite serious, my friend, when I ask you what will you sell me that horse for."

Then says the other, " Well, give me what it is worth."

" Suppose I give you ten thousand piastres."

" Nay," said the peasant to himself, " did I not say he was laughing at me ? and now he talks of giving me ten thousand piastres. Well, but I'll have my joke at his expense." So he replies again, " As much as it is worth."

" I'll give you twenty, thirty, fifty thousand piastres," says the Prince.

By this time the poor peasant lost patience, and said, " Come, give me the fifty thousand and take it."

Then the Prince pays him down the fifty thousand piastres, and takes the horse, and afterwards takes from him his dress and puts it on, and gives him his own for it and says, " Now get you home."

The poor fellow still thought he was making fun of him, and sat still.

" My good fellow," says the other, " get along with you ; those things are yours."

Then he sets off on his way, and from time to time turned and looked back to see whether they were not pursuing him, for he still could not believe that the money and clothes were his. He came to his home attired like a king. His wife sees him and does not know him and tries to drive him away. "Why, wife," says he, "I am your husband."

She begins to tear her hair and cry, "Alack! alack! woe's me! my husband has turned Turk."

"Tush, wife," says he. "Be quiet, we have made our fortune."

And then he proceeds to tell her how it all happened. So the peasant came to be the first squire in the village, with houses, and estates, and vineyards, and had an easy time of it.

But let us now come back to the Prince, whom the mare bade kill the horse and take off its skin, but give good heed that it received no damage anywhere. So he slays the horse and takes off the skin without making a rent in any part of it. And then she bids him wrap her up in that skin, so that our fine mare had the appearance of the lame horse, and her rider only that of a peasant. Then she tells him when they come into the town that he is to go to the butcher's and get a bladder and clap it on his head, so that he would look like a man with a scab-pate, and no one should know him.

Accordingly, when they entered his father's town he took a bladder and clapped it, all uncleaned as it was, on the top of his head, and was the funniest looking object in the world. Then he mounts on his horse and goes to the place where his father the King was living, and where there were so many princes come to try their luck at the wager.

When the people saw him they were like to split for laughter, and cry out to him, "Why you dear mangey old man, here are all these sons of kings and viziers throwing their lives away—as their hearts might tell even the beasts they ride on—and you come here with your wretched lame old hack, and offer to enter the lists with them!"

However, that was the wager, it was open to high and low. So he obtains leave to go, and goes to the lake; and the hack gives a bit of a neigh, and takes a jump and clears the lake, and thence gives another leap and comes back again to the place where she was before.

The King and the rest rolled their eyes in wonder, when they saw how the scab-pate, whom they were laughing at, had won the wager and gained the Princess. The King was ready to burst with vexation at having to take such an object for his son-in-law, and said, "Whoever calls him my son-in-law, I will cut off his head."

And he rushes off to the palace and reproaches the Princess with her ill luck, because so many princes and dukes had come after her, and none had been able to win the wager but this dirty, mangey old fellow. And he kicks her down stairs and puts her down in the barn, and orders the cook to give her just enough to eat to keep her alive.

The poor Queen, when she saw that, was full of sorrow and grief; she went and reasoned with him:

"What fault is it of the poor girl's?"

But he drew his sword to smite her. However, when she had left him, she went down and comforted the girl, and made a couch for her with coverlids, and whatever else she wanted, and went to the cook, and told him to give her daughter plenty to eat, and not to mind what the King said. And had it not been for her mother, the poor girl would have died from her misery. Well in the evening, the scab-pate too entered the barn; but the Princess would not turn round to look at him, and when they lay down, he put the sword betwixt them, and they slept like brother and sister, as, in fact, they were. The day dawns, and the mother asks her how she got on with the scab-pate, and she tells her, "It is not enough for him to be that, but he must be proud as well."

And how should she know he was her brother? In five or six days a king, who had lost a son in the wager, declared war, and the forces mustered to fight. Then the scab-pate tells the Princess to inform her father that, if he is willing, he will go to the war.

"Why," says she, "how can I go and appear before my father, he might kill me?"

"Tell your mother, then," said he, "and let her tell him."

So the girl told it her mother, and she tells the King, who answers her:

"What! haven't I told you a thousand times never to mention the fellow's name to me? If he's not sick of it by the time it comes to fighting, let him go!"

For he wished him to be killed, so as to get rid of him. Then
the mother goes and tells him, " The King says you are to go to
the war too."

So he arose the same day that the army were to march, and
mounted his horse ; and as he went forward at the head of the
soldiers, with the King and all the great ones of the land, he
came to a puddle, and tumbled into it with his lame horse, and
struggled, and struggled, but could not get up again. The King,
for very shame, turned his face another way, and the others bit
their lips, for they were ashamed, and afraid of the King besides,
and said to themselves :

" Ah, the King was proud, and therefore God sent him such a
son-in-law as it makes him burn with shame to look on."

The army goes on, and he is still left sticking in the mud. At
length he gets up, and goes to a little hill, and takes off the skin
from his mare, and takes soap, and gives himself a good wash,
and puts on the saddle which is like the sky, and the stars, and
the corresponding suit of clothes, and mounts the steed, and the
mare flies like the wind and descends to the plain, and he goes under
a tree and dismounts, and sits down. Forthwith the King sends
messengers, and begs him to come to his tent ; but he does not
stir from his place. The King comes himself and salutes him,
and embraces him, and entreats him to come to his tent that he
may entertain him. But he replies :

" I have only come here to look on: I am not a fighting
man."

Then the King departs, and goes and sends him a number of
presents. In a little while the battle begins, and he sees how his
father's forces are being destroyed, and the enemy are now
about to take him prisoner. Then he could abide it no longer,
but drew his sword, and mounted his horse, and rushed into the
battle, and hewed and hacked among the foreign troops, until he
fell in with their King, whom he captured, and brought to his
father. And he begged them to spare his life, and offered to pay
them tribute. So they let him live. Then his father falls and
embraces his son, and covers him with kisses, saying :

" Ah, my saviour and deliverer of my land, come, let us go to
the palace, and you shall be King, and I will be your slave."

M

And, as he was speaking to him, the mare flies away, and they lose him from sight ; and then, indeed, the King exclaims :

"It is no man, but an angel of God : and it seems I must have done some good deed, in reward for which he has sent him to deliver me."

And they arise and come to the town with music and rejoicings. Meanwhile, our friend, the Prince, went up on to the hill, and took off the fine clothes, and donned again those of the scab-pate, and went and tumbled into the mud, and pretended that he had not yet been able to get up. The others see him, and begin to laugh, and say, "Alas! poor scab-pate, we have been and fought and conquered, and come back again; and you, you precious villain, are still in the mud!"

But he answered never a word. They come into town, and the Queen asked after the scab-pate, who was so anxious to be killed, and they tell her he is still sticking in the mud. Afterwards the King comes, and tells her about the Prince, who came to his rescue in the battle, and said :

"Ah, my dear wife, would that I had such a son-in-law, instead of a scab-pate ; I would give my life for him."

Then the mother went and told her daughter ; and thereupon. the Princess says :

"He ought to have a present. Let us just embroider him a golden turban, and make him a present of it next time he comes out to battle," and she immediately engages workwomen and they began to embroider the splendid head-dress.

A few days afterwards another king declares war ; and, to make a short story of it, the same thing happened as before : the scab pate fell again into the mire, then he went, put on his second suit —this time the sea with the fishes—and went down to the plain again, and conquered the foe, and again went and tumbled in the mud. Once more the King came and told the Queen about the hero, and said to her :

"If it had not been for him, we should all have been sold into. slavery."

In five or six days later there was another war, greater than the rest. By that time the golden turban was ready : so the Queen takes it, and brings it to the King, and says :

" Here is the golden turban, which you must give to the hero who helps you."

And the King was exceedingly pleased. The same things happened in that war as had happened in the former ones. However, this time he did not at once descend to the plain, but only after three days, and now he acted so that his father's blood nearly congealed in his veins for fear—for all his hopes hung on the issue—and at the end of the three days, when his father was all but taken prisoner, he put on his third change of raiment —the green fields with the flowers—and descended into the plain. Then indeed was the time when he caused great mourning, for while his mare slew and devoured some, he dispatched others. But there was one warrior who wounded him in the hand, so that the blood flowed. And the King, who was near him, forthwith took out the golden turban and wrapped it round his hand. And they continued the fight until they had taken the other King, and him, too, they forced to pay tribute.

Then once more the mare rushed from their midst, with the Prince ; but he went no more to tumble in the mire. And the troops returned in triumph and joy, because they had won all the battles. But they owed their victory to the scab-pate. They came to the mud. There is no scab-pate to be seen, and they declare that the scab-pate has got the happy dispatch in that battle, and they go and bring the news to the Queen and to the Princess, and they too rejoice. But that evening, when night fell, behold our friend the Prince mounted on his golden mare, in his rich attire, appears, with his sword, and goes into the barn and finds the Princess, who at the sight of such a comely hero is beside herself with admiration, and at once recognises him for the same man of whom her mother had told her ; and she at once regained her spirits, and began to laugh as her brother conversed with her.

Now the King heard the laughter of his daughter, and was wroth, and said, "The scab-pate is fondling her, and she dares to giggle ! She fancies she has got a Prince before her." But she kept on laughing until he got into a towering rage, and took his sword and went to slay her. Then the Queen falls on his neck, and says to him, "In God's name, what are about ?

Who knows? she may be laughing from excess of grief?" So they send the maidservant to tell her to be quiet. The maid goes and beholds the mare with the Prince, and stands aghast, and keeps gazing, and never returns to bring back any tidings. Then the King is angry indeed, and seizes his sword and goes to kill all four of them; but when he comes into their presence, he beholds in the barn his deliverer instead of the poor scab-pate. Then he flings away his sword and falls on his neck and covers him with kisses. "Ah, my life and soul!" he exclaims, "have you deigned to enter the barn? Come let us go upstairs."

"No," he replies; "to-night I will stay here, but I will come to-morrow."

So they sat for some time laughing and joking, and at length the King bids them good night, and departs, and goes up-stairs and orders them to prepare the palace, and spread fresh dine branches everywhere, for to-morrow he means to keep his daughter's wedding.

And below, the Prince was laughing and joking all night long with the Princess.

Early in the morning the King rises and brings him upstairs, lifted aloft by his slave, so that his feet might not touch the ground, and goes and calls his council and all his grandees and friends to his daughter's wedding. When they were all assembled they spread the tables for the feast. And the Prince goes to wash himself, and then the King, in his joy at getting such a son-in-law, takes the towel on his shoulder, and the jug in his hand and goes and pours out water, and the Prince washes himself. The Prince stood there; and he poured out the water for him to wash, in order that his dream might be fulfilled. Then they sat down at table, and the eyes of all were fastened on the Prince.

When they had finished eating, the Prince addresses them as follows: "Sirs, I am going to tell you a tale; but I must insist that no one interrupts me in my story."

All shouted with one voice, "No, no! noble Prince!"

Then he began and related the story which we have told. When the King heard the words, "There was once a King who had three sons, and he told them to go to sleep, and to tell him what each one dreamt"—he called out, "I am the King who did that !" "Nay, but I beg," said the Prince, "that you will not interrupt my story. Well," he continued, "two of his sons had a dream, and at once he divided with them their inheritance. The youngest of all cried that he had not had any dream . . . . ." Again the King was unable to keep silence, and said, "Why, my good sir ! that's what happened to me !"

Then the council said to him, "Nay but, oh King, your mother bore with you for nine months, and you cannot bear one hour with the young man's story ! "

Then the King again was silent, and the Prince goes on with his tale, telling how the youngest, who said he had no dream, had indeed had one, but feared to tell it, because he had seen how his father had poured out water for him to wash ; "And what does that mean, my lords ? " he asked. They reply that it meant that he would turn out better than his father. "That was the reason," he continued, " why he feared he would kill him ; and so he said he had seen nothing. Wherefore he thought him a luckless wight, and gave him to the executioner to slay, and required as a token his little finger. And if you don't believe—look there ! I am the Prince in question." And he showed his little finger ; and he added further, "I too am the scab-pate, whom you ridicule ! " And therewith he falls on the neck of the executioner and embraces him (for he too was at the table), and he says to him, "You are my father, for you saved my life ! " And he gives him a present and made him grand vizier. Then indeed, there were great rejoicings, now that he that had been slain was found. And afterwards the Princess was married, and the Prince married also and they lived a very happy life, and we a happier one still.

CONSTANTES AND THE DRAGON.

(TENOS.)

------:c:------

ONCE on a time there was an old man who had three sons, and all three determined to go and learn a trade. So they went out among the uplands to find work, and as they were sojourning there they found a field unreapt, and said to each other, "Come brothers, let us go in and reap it, and whoever it is he will pay us." So they set to and reaped, and while they were reaping they saw the mountains trembling and beheld a dragon coming, and they said to each other, "Come, brothers, let's work away, for here comes the owner."

When the dragon comes up, he said, "Good morrow to you, my lads."

"Good morrow, master," they answered.

"What are you doing there?" They said, "We found the field unreapt, and went in to reap it, for we said, 'Whoever it belongs to will pay us.'"

When they had reaped half of it, the dragon said to the youngest, whom they called Constantes, "Do you see yonder mountain? There lives my wife, the dragoness. You see this letter, take it to her."

So Constantes took the letter, but he was a cunning fellow, and as he went along it struck him he might as well open the letter and read it. So he opened the letter and it ran as follows: "The man I send you you must slaughter, and put in the oven and cook so as to have him ready for me to gobble up to-night when I come home."

So he tore up the letter, and wrote another as follows. "My dear dragoness,—When the bearer of this arrives, I beg you to kill the best turkey for him, and stuff it, and fill him a basket

with loaves, and send him here with food for the labourers."
When the dragon saw from afar Constantes returning with his
beast of burden laden, he said:

"Ah, that fellow is a cleverer rogue then I! Come, friends,
let's get out of this quickly, and go to supper this evening at my
house, that I may pay you!"

So they finished their reaping, and the dragon took them away
with him. On their way, the little Constantes said to his
brothers:

"Ho, brothers! you have four eyes among you. Let us keep
wide awake at the place where we are going."

At night, when the dragon and his wife had gone to sleep, Constantes gets up and wakes his brothers, and goes softly up to the
dragoness and takes her ring from her finger, and takes his
brothers with him and makes off, and within an hour or two they
are in the town. The dragon wakes up and looks for the men to
eat them. Then the dragoness sees that her ring is gone from
her finger, and says:

"Why dragon! my ring is gone!"

So the dragon arose and mounted his horse, and went in search
of them. As he was riding along, he spied them before him
approaching the confines of the town, and called after them:

"Constantes, stop and let me pay you!"

But they reply that they want no pay.

Again the dragon calls to them, "Come back!"

But they return no answer, and thus they reach the town.
They come right into it, and commence business, the eldest as a
draper, the second as a carpenter, and Constantes, the youngest,
as a tailor. The eldest brother was jealous of the youngest,
because he had the ring, and he wished to kill him.

So he goes and says to the King:

"Please your Majesty, you have plenty of good things, but if
you had but the diamond coverlid of the dragon in your palace,
you would be alone among the monarchs of the earth."

Says the King, "But how am I to get it? Who is able to fetch
it for me?"

Then he answered, "Let your Majesty issue a proclamation
saying, that whoever will fetch the dragon's coverlid, you will

make a great and mighty man of him. Then send and summon my youngest brother, who is a tailor, and tell him to go and get it for you, and if he refuses, threaten to destroy him."

Accordingly the King issued a proclamation, but no one was found who dared to go. Then he sends a summons by his vizier to Constantes, and tells him to go and bring the diamond coverlid of the dragon, and threatens to destroy him if he refuses. What could Constantes do? He set out on his journey, and said:

"May the blessing of my mother and my sire stand me in good stead!"

So he journeyed forth and went on his way, and as he went he met an old woman, and said to her:

"Good morrow, mother."

"The same to you, my son!" says she. "Whither away? Whoever goes this way never comes back again."

Says he, "The King has sent me to go and fetch him the diamond coverlid of the dragon."

"Alas! my son, you will be lost!"

"But what can I do?" he answers.

"Go back and tell those who sent you to give you three reeds, the one to be filled with lice, the other with bugs, and the other with fleas, and you must to the back of the house by night, when the dragon is asleep, and quietly make a hole in the wall, and empty the reeds upon the dragon's bed. Then the dragon and the dragoness will not be able to endure all these insects, and they will seize the coverlid and fling it out of the window, and leave it hanging there. Then you must seize the coverlid and make off as fast as you can, for if the dragon catches you, he will eat you."

So the lad did all the old woman had told him, and took the coverlid and ran off with it. Now let us leave Constantes for a time, and come to the dragon, who got up and found the coverlid missing.

"Why dragoness! what's become of the coverlid?" he said.

"I don't know," said the dragoness.

"Ah, wife," said the dragon, "no one can have taken it but Constantes." Then he goes down to his stable, and chooses out his best horse, mounts it, and in an hour or two comes up with Constantes, and says to him :

"Give me the coverlid ! What trick have you been playing me, you dog ? "

Constantes replies, "What I have done so far is nothing: wait what I shall do to you soon."

The dragon could not get at Constantes, for he was on the borders of the King's territory, so he had to return. Constantes brought the coverlid to the King, and the King ordered them to cut him two suits of clothes ; so Constantes went his way. After the lapse of twenty days, the eldest brother went to the King and said :

" King, has Constantes brought you the coverlid ? "

And the King answered, " Yes, and a very fine one it is."

" Ah, your Majesty," he said, " but if you had the horse and the bell which belong to the dragon, you would have nothing more to desire."

So the King issued another proclamation, and no one was found who dared to go.

Then Constantes' employer called him, and said, " Constantes, the King wants you." So Constantes goes to the King, who says to him :

" You must go and fetch me the horse and bell that belong to the dragon, and if you don't go, I shall kill you."

What was poor Constantes to do ?

He went away and pondered how he was to obtain the horse and the bell, for the horse would neigh, and the bell would ring, and the dragon would wake and come down and eat him.

But what could he do against the King's command ? So he sets off on his journey. As he travelled, he again met the same old woman whom he had met before.

" Good day," says he.

"The same to you, my son," says she. " Whither away again ? "

"Don't ask me !" he says. "The King has sent me to bring him the dragon's horse and bell, and if I don't go he will kill me."

Then the old woman said to him, " Go down to town and tell them to give you forty-one plugs, for the bell has forty-one holes ; and then make haste hence to the dragon's den, and when you arrive at night, lose no time in stopping all the holes in the bell, for if you leave one unstopped it will ring, and the dragon will come out to eat you. But in that case, as soon as you hear the bell ring, you must run and hide yourself in the barn among the chaff, and the dragon will come and call, 'I smell man's flesh,' but you must be concealed among the chaff, and when you hear that he is gone upstairs again, you must plug the remaining hole, and take the horse and mount it, and put the bell on it, and fly."

Constantes did all that the old woman told him, so he got the bell and the horse, and ran away with them. The dragon immediately mounts another horse and comes up with Constantes, close to the borders of the King's land. He calls to him :

"You villain, bring me my horse and bell, and I will do you no harm."

But Constantes replies, "What I have done so far is nothing : wait what I will do to you next."

Then the dragon ran ; and Constantes ran, so that the dragon could not catch him, and Constantes came to the King and brought him the horse and the bell. So the King cut him two more suits, and Constantes went off about his business.

After twenty days more the eldest brother went again to the King and asked him, saying, "Oh, King, has my brother brought you the horse and bell ? "

And the King answered, "Yes."

"Ah, your Majesty ! now you've got everything else : but if you had the dragon himself to exhibit, then you would want nothing more."

So the King issued a proclamation, "Whoever is able to bring me the dragon, that I may show him in public, I will give him a large kingdom."

Then his employer came and said to Constantes : "Do you hear how they are sending word for you, to go and fetch the dragon?"

And Constantes said, "How can I go and fetch the dragon, who will then make an end of me any way ? "

But his master said, "You cannot refuse to go."

So the lad arose and went his way. And as he went he met the same old woman again ; and said to her, "Good morrow, mother."

" Good day, my son ! Whither away this time ? "

" I am going to fetch the dragon, for if I don't bring him the King will kill me. And I wish you would tell me what to do, for now I am sure I shall lose my life."

Then she answered him, " Don't be dismayed ; but go back and tell the King they must provide you with a tattered suit : a hatchet, and a saw, an awl, ten nails and four ropes. And when he has given you these things, you must go the place and put on the tattered garments and begin to hew the plane-tree, which is outside the dragon's castle. And he, when he hears the noise, will come out to you, and say, ' Good day to you ! What are you labouring away at there, old man ? ' ' What do you think, my friend ? ' you must answer, ' I am working at a coffin for Constantes, who has died, and I have been at work all this time, and can't cut the tree down.' "

Then Constantes went back and got all the necessaries, and went close outside the dragon's castle, and began to hew away at the plane-tree. The dragon heard the noise, and came out and said to him :

" What are you doing here, old man ? "

" I am working at a coffin for Constantes," he replied ; " Constantes, the man who has just died, and I can't cut the plane-tree down."

At this the dragon was so pleased that he said, " Ah, the dog ! I'll soon manage it."

So when the old man, and the dragon had nailed the coffin together between them, the former said to the latter, " Get in and let's see whether it's right. For you are the same size as he."

So the dragon got into the coffin, and lay down on his face : but the old man said, " Turn on your back, I can't see your figure properly."

So the dragon turned his face uppermost, and the old man got up to try on the lid, to see whether it fitted, and when he had put it on, he nailed it down and tied it tight ; and he had his horse hidden behind a wall ; and went and brought the horse, and tied the dragon on its back and rode off with him.

Then the dragon began to call out, " Old man, let me out : for the coffin fits ! "

But the old man answered him, "Constantes has got you right and tight now, and is taking you to the King, that he may exhibit you in public!"

So he carried off the coffin and brought it to the King and said, "Now I have brought him to you, take care of him, and fetch my eldest brother to open the coffin."

The next day the eldest brother came and asked the King if Constantes had brought the dragon, and the King answered him, "Yes!"

Then he said to the King, "Well, as he has brought you the dragon, he can bring you the dragoness' diamond ring."

So the King issued yet another proclamation, to the effect that whoever was able to bring him the dragoness' diamond ring, he would give him a great kingdom. But no one was found who would venture.

Then again the employer of Constantes says to him, "In order to be quit of the affair, you must yet go and fetch the diamond ring of the dragoness, that they may leave you in peace."

Then said the lad, "Well, as my fate so wills it, I may as well go!"

And he set forth upon his errand; and on his way he again met the old woman, and wished her good day.

"The same to you, my son," she answers. "What brings you this way again?"

"Oh, don't ask me!" he answers. "They have sent me once more—this time for the dragoness' ring. What am I to do?"

"I'll tell you what to do," says she. "You must forge a letter, and write as follows: 'Dragoness, you are to kill the bearer, and put him in the oven and bake him, and hang his feet outside the gate; and when I come back I will eat him.'"

So Constantes went and saluted her thus:

"Good day to you, Mistress Dragon!"

"The same to you, young man. What is your pleasure?"

"Here is a letter for you which the dragon gave me."

The dragoness read the letter and said, "Sit down, young man while I make ready."

So the dragoness went away and proceeded to prepare the oven, and when she had got it ready she called Constantes and said, "Come, get up on that shovel, and cast a shadow that we may judge whether the oven is hot enough."

So Constantes pretended to get up, and kept tumbling down again, which he did on purpose. At length he said to the dragoness, "Do you go up, and show me how to do it, for I don't know."

So the dragoness got up to show Constantes the way; but Constantes was cunning, and when the dragoness got up on to the shovel to show him, he gave her a push, and flung her into the oven, and took and cut off her two breasts and hung them outside the gate, and took the ring from her finger, and then departed.

When he had given it to the King, he said to him, "Now, please your Majesty, it is time to open the coffin and exhibit the dragon for the enjoyment of your Majesty and all the people. But call my eldest brother to open it."

Then the King summoned the eldest brother of Constantes to come and open the coffin, in order to take the dragon out. Meanwhile all the people were gathered at casement and balcony to look at the dragon.

So the eldest brother came, and opened the coffin to fetch out the dragon. And when he had opened it, the dragon, seeing such a crowd at the casements and balconies, but no one else near him except the man who had opened the lid, swallowed him at a gulp. Then the King let the dragon go, and the dragon ran off home. The first thing he saw when he reached the gate was the two breasts hanging there. He goes in and looks for the dragoness, but cannot find her. At last he goes down to the oven and opens it, and sees the dragoness inside burnt to a cinder.

THE CRAZY PRIESTESS WITH HER CRAZY DAUGHTERS.

(Astypalæa.)

————:o:————

Once on a time there was a priest who had a wife and three daughters. But I must tell you that all four of them were an even match for each other in point of folly. One day, the eldest daughter, the pride of the family, went outside the town, as soon as church was over, to take a walk. She espies a steep cliff, and at once goes forward and sits on the edge of the cliff, and begins to weep and wail:

"Alas, to think that I shall marry, and have a little child, and he shall come and look over here, and fall over the edge, and get killed. Alas, my darling, my darling!"

The others were waiting for her, and said, "Why, what can have become of our sister?"

The second one goes to fetch her, and sees her sitting on a rock, and lamenting.

"My dear," she says, "what's the matter with you that you weep?"

"Alas!" replies the other, "don't you see this steep cliff? where—when I am married, and get a little nephew for you, he'll come and tumble down, and be killed?"

Then the other sits down and cries. Lastly, they send the youngest of all. She, too, does the same; so, to avoid repetition, we will add, the mother also comes and bewails the sad fate of her grandson.

The worthy priest runs to look for them, and finds the good women weeping and wailing. When he asks them what's the matter that they are crying in this fashion, they reply that the eldest daughter is going to marry and have a little baby, and it will tumble down that steep cliff!

He replies, "Bless me! bad luck take you all! how long am

I to put up with your folly. You never will learn sense! Heaven is my witness that I will get away from here, and leave you to your fate, or you will be the death of me."

So he packs up and departs, saying to them, " If fortune is kind to you, you most unhappy women, and I chance to find any who are worse fools than you, it may be I shall see you again ; otherwise your eyes will lose their lustre, ere ever you look on me again."

Then the priest journeys on and on, until he comes to another village, and in a certain house he hears lamentations, and peeps in to see what is going on ; and beholds a woman who had a child in a cradle, and over it against a wall there was a hatchet hanging, and she did nothing but cry :

" Alack ! my baby, my baby, killed by a hatchet ! "

"Good woman," says the priest, addressing her, "what are you weeping about ? "

" Why, don't you see, your reverence, that that hatchet will fall and kill my child ? And you ask me why I am weeping ? "

" Ah, then I'm not the only one ! " said the priest to himself; and added aloud, " What will you give me to save it from so sad a fate ? "

" Whatever you please, your reverence ; my very life, if it was my own to give ! "

Thereupon, he moves the cradle to another part of the room. " There, good woman," he says, " now don't cry any more."

Then the good priest receives a handsome fee, and travels further, and soon he comes to a place where he sees a crowd gathered. There were shouts and lamentations. So the priest went to see what was up. And what should he behold but a tall man who was to be married, and the door of the house was rather low, and he would not stoop to enter. But they were considering what they should do, whether they should cut off his feet or his head. For these seemed the only alternatives. At this sight the priest shook his sides with laughter, and then addressed them thus :

" Fellow Christians, what ails you that you weep ? "

Then they explain to him the state of the case. "Oh," says he, " I'll get him in for you. What will you give me ? "

" Take whatever you will. Only do us that favour ? "

Then the priest takes hold of his head. "Stoop a bit, my son,"
he says, "a little more, a little more," he repeated, until he got
him in. Then said he, " There ! now lift up your head again, and
as often as you go in and out, you must do the same; do you
see ? "

Then he takes and marries him into the bargain, after which he
takes leave of the company, and goes further. Some way on he
sees an old woman who had a sow, which she was washing and
decking with diamonds and spangles to go to the wedding; for
this, said she, was her daughter.

At length she espies the priest. "Oh, my son," she cries, "pray
take my girl to the wedding, for you see I am old and can't go ;
I'll pay you for the trouble of walking so far ? "

" Willingly, mother, I shall regard it as a favour to myself," he
replied; and here again he had an eye to the main chance. So
the good priest takes the sow and drives it on before him. But
when he had gone a little way, the old woman seemed uneasy, for
she called after the priest :

" Oh, my son, turn round and let me look at you, that I may
know you again ? "

Whereupon the good priest, without more ado, presented his
back to her.

"Oh, thank you, thank you !" she cried. "What a handsome
round face, and what expressive features ! Yes, now I shall know
you again. Only please bring me a cake from the feast ! "

When the priest had turned the corner, he stripped the sow
and took all the gold and silver ornaments, and thus laden with
treasures he returned to his wife.

" Welcome home, father," they cried, "where have you been
wandering all this long time ? Why we were almost in despair ? "

" I thought," said he, " there were none like you in the world ;
but, as I see, there are others who outstrip you. Henceforth I
shall put up with you for better, for worse."

And with the profits he brought home he got his daughters
dowered and married, and lived happily with his wife ever after,
although she did play a mad freak or two from time to time. And
may we be happier still.

THE MAN WITHOUT A BEARD.

(TENOS.)

——:o:——

GOOD evening to your lord and ladyships!

There was once a beardless man, who had a wife, who asked him to get her some new cheese. So Mr. Beardless meets a shepherd on the road, and asks him whether he has any fresh cheese?

"No, my poor smooth-face, indeed I have not, and know not how to get it. For no sooner do I milk my sheep and curdle the milk, than there comes along a dragon and steals the curds, and eats them, and it's a long time since I made anything of the sort, may the curse of Christ light on the brute."

"Is that a true story and no lie? Then I am the man who will avenge you of the dragon. As soon as you have milked your ewes, and set the milk to curdle, call me!"

The poor shepherd answered, "If you will but rid me of him, I will bring you plenty of milk and cheese gratis, and will be thankful to you ever afterwards."

When the hour drew near, the dragon prepared again to visit the shepherd's fold. The Beardless One went earlier, and shut himself in and stood at the entrance, and looked out for the dragon's arrival. He put some live ashes before the door, and strewed them on the ground. Then he takes some of the curds in his hands, and put on iron shoes with nails underneath. When the dragon comes, he looks round on the side he was accustomed to enter, to see whether the shepherd had made his curds, that he might come in and eat them. Then the Man without a Beard, shouts to him:

"Who are you?"

And the dragon answers, "A dragon!"

"Dragon, indeed," says the other; "why you seem like a fly to me, and you call yourself a dragon."

The dragon now tried to enter, but the other, who was looking through the opening, cried,

"Ah, ill-fated dragon, I swear by this stone, which drops water when I squeeze it, and by this earth which vomits fire when I tread on it, that I will swallow you through the opening, for you're but as a fly in my eyes."

The poor dragon was terribly frightened, and said, "Let us be brothers from henceforward."

Whereupon they at once make friends. The shepherd from that time had his milk and cheese to himself, and the dragon followed the Man without a Beard.

The dragon said, "Let us go a-hunting, and cook and eat. Do you take one way, and I the other, and we will see who brings home most."

As the Beardless One was walking along he espied a wild boar, who tried to gore him with his tusks. The poor fellow was in great distress, so he climbed up a tree, and the boar tried to rend the tree with his tusks, and to fling the Beardless One down. But in his efforts to break down the tree, he got his tusks so firmly fixed in the trunk that he died and hung dead upon the tree.

Then the Beardless One sees that the wild boar is dead and comes down from the tree. He considers a moment, and then runs to find the dragon.

"Dragon," he shouts, "come here; come and see what I have caught. Have you caught anything yet?"

"I have not found anything at present," replied the dragon. "And you?"

"Oh, just a trifle of a pigling that I have caught and fastened to the tree. Go you, and fetch it for us to cook, and I'll come directly."

This he said, because he was quite unable to lift such a heavy wild boar, so this was why he excused himself. The dragon took the boar and skinned it, and when the Beardless One came up, the dragon said:

"Well, what are you doing? Where have you been all this

time ; go and fill this skin with water, and bring it, that we may dress and cook the beast."

The Beardless One took the skin and filled it with water. Then he tries to lift it, but in vain. Thereupon he begins to thump the full skin with a stick, and to call out himself, "Oh, oh, oh ! who is beating me ?"

The dragon hears the shouts and thumps, and runs to see what the Beardless One is after all this time.

Then the Beardless One says to him, "See, you've missed them. Some ten rascals came to carry off our water, and I gave them a thrashing, and killed some and lamed others, and they ran away. Take up this skin with the water in it, and I'll go after them and give them another thrashing, for I took pity on them, and now I'm sorry I let them off so easily."

The dragon believed him, and said :

" Oh, my good fellow, let them alone, now ; I'll take the skin of water, and do you go and fetch wood to cook with, for I'm hungry."

" All right, I'll go ; but give me a long rope to tie them up with."

So he goes off and ties the rope round about ten trees, and pulls at them, crying, " Pull-y-oh, haul-y-oh ! "

When the dragon found he was so long in returning, he went to find him. He sees him in the distance with the rope round the trees, beckoning to him not to speak.

" Hush, hush ! " he whispered. The dragon was amazed, and cried, " Look at the madman ! He can't lift one, and he wants ten ! "

" You stupid dragon ! " says the other, " I told you not to speak, and not to come near me. Now see what you've done."

Then the Beardless One works himself into a passion, and says to the dragon :

" There, now, I was going to bring the whole hill as it stands, with all the trees on it, to your den. But as you wouldn't get out of the way, and would come and talk to me, you may now do as you please. I won't consent to lift a single tree. I am like to lose the prowess I inherited from my sire."

And the dragon believed him. But the Man without a Beard

tried every device to escape from the dragon, for he saw he should not get on well with him.

The dragon pulls up a tree by the roots, takes it on his shoulder, and departs. When he reached home, he cooked the dinner, and sat down, and ate. Then it struck him that the Man without a Beard was a humbug, and he thought he would put him to the test. So he said to him, " My Beardless friend, what say you, shall we go and have a wrestling bout in the market place, and see which can master the other ? "

" We will," said he.

So they set off, and on the way they begin to fight, and, with a single push from the dragon, the Beardless One falls to the ground.

" Ah, Beardless, where's the valour that you have from your sire ? " said the dragon.

" Why, you silly dragon, I slipped," said his companion.

Another push, and down goes Beardless again, with the dragon kneeling on top of him.

" Ha, Beardless," says he, "where's your sire's valour now ? How you roll your eyes ! "

" Roll my eyes," says the Beardless One (for his eyes were starting from their sockets with the weight of the dragon on his chest), "yes, I'm rolling my eyes, and considering whither I shall throw you, whether to the east or to the west, for you are just like a fly to me."

Again the dragon believes him, and gets up, and cries, " No, no, my brother (for are we not brothers ?), don't throw me anywhere ; only teach me, too, how your sire made such a hero of you ! "

" Come along," says he, " and I'll tell you."

Then the Beardless One begins as follows :

" My father buried me in the earth, digging a deep hole, and said to me, ' Now, jump.' But as I could not jump out, he told me to turn my ear towards him, and he let a drop of water trickle in it, and told me to say, as the water trickled in ' Wobble-ty-wob, wobble-ty-wob, wobble-ty-wob,' and then I began to gain my strength, and succeeded in jumping out of the hole, which before was much too deep for me."

The dragon wished to acquire the same strength, and so the Man without a Beard began to dig a deep hole. Then he said to the dragon, " Get in," and the dragon got in.

" Jump," he cried, and the dragon jumped out immediately.

Then said the Beardless One, " I must dig it deeper."

And when he had dug it again, and the dragon could no longer leap such a height, the Beardless One said to him :

" Now turn your ear towards me, and I'll dribble the water in, and you must say, ' Wobble-ty-wob.' "

Now the Beardless One had some boiling water at hand. The dragon turned up his ear, and the Beardless One at first let fall a tiny little drop into his ear from the edge of the hole. The dragon kept saying, "Wobble-ty-wob;" but after a time the water scalded him so severely, that he called out, " Oh, Beardless, Beardless !" and instead of saying, " Wobble-ty-wob, wobble-ty-wob, my master," he began to say, " Bobble-ty-bob, Bobble-ty-bob, my Beardless," till he died, and there was an end of him, for the water was scalding hot, and he could not jump out. So at last he understood that the Beardless One had cheated him; and thus the former got rid of the dragon. Then the Man without a Beard departed, and went to find the shepherd.

" Now," said he, " that I have rid you of the dragon, what will you give me ? "

" Whatever you please. One of my best ewes. Go out and pick for yourself," said the shepherd. So the Beardless One takes a fine fat ewe, and sets off home in haste. On the way there comes a fox, and runs off with his ewe. The Beardless One gives chase to her, but the fox goes and hides in her hole. The Beardless One could not get into the hole. So he considered, and said, " You shall see, Madame Reynard (Madame Reynard was the name of the fox) how I'll manage you."

So he takes a pair of gourds and hangs them on a stick over the hole of the fox. A strong north wind blew, and the gourds sighed in the breeze, and called out, "Whoo, whoo, whoo." The fox thought it was the Man without a Beard, and gnawed away at the ewe, in her hole, tortured with thirst, without daring to come out. But, at length, she said, " Sooner than perish with thirst, I might as well go out, and see what is moaning like that." Instead of the Beardless One, she sees the gourds, and ties them to her tail, in a rage, and takes them to throw them into the sea. When she attempted to turn round, to fling the gourds from her, they overbalanced her, and she fell into the sea, gourds and all, and they pulled her down ; so Madame Reynard was drowned and the tale is finished.

FINIS.